Autistic Psychedelic Community

This book is dedicated to every single person who ever took the time to offer their words or time or expertise or resources or any other form of support to the Autistic Psychedelic Community. Many of those who've contributed to our mission have done so without expecting anything in return apart from knowing that their generosity would be carried forward. And it is because of such kindness that this community has been able to serve & support so many others around the world in so many meaningful ways...

By purchasing this text, you're also becoming one such supporter.
So, thank you. Really.

Learn More & Support
The Autistic Psychedelic Community Project

To more fully understand the concepts contained in this book, please read or listen to these other great books published by Neurotopia Press — available as books, audiobooks & e-books via the APC supporter shop @ AutisticPsychedelic.com/support

How To Open
QR-Coded Links:

1. Open Camera App
2. Hover Over Code
3. Tap Popup Link :)

GIANT DISCLAIMER BECAUSE WE CARE

This book in no way encourages *anyone*, under *any* circumstances, to engage in *any* form of self-medication nor the utilization of *any* illicit substances for any purpose whatsoever. Period. Exclamation marks ! ! !

Similarly, if anyone reading this sentence right now is considering the use of psychedelic molecules for the purposes of inducing psychedelic states or engendering other *potential* personal health benefits, it is CRITICAL that we *STILL* recommend that all seekers similarly seek the informed guidance of trusted, trained professionals....

No one needs to navigate this alone. No one needs to do this work unsupported. And if anyone is interested in learning about or engaging with any form of psychedelic practice, it is CRITICAL that we once again point out that there is a great big world of professionals who are capable and willing to foster that curiosity **if** and **when** such an exploration has been deemed safe by someone who is qualified to make that particular determination......

We get it. Psychedelics sure do seem interesting, yeah? We hear about them on the news. We see the research coming out from major academic institutions. Great. But that doesn't mean *any* of us need to take on any risks that we could otherwise mitigate through the seeking of proper education, screenings, supervision, and support.....

No matter how helpful psychedelics may be, there's no substitute for healthy habits, patience, compassion, love, gratitude, and community. So please... Be safe. Thanks!....

— Introduction —

Hi. My name is Aaron Paul Orsini and I am the Director of Peer Support, Education, and Research for the Autistic Psychedelic Community (APC). The APC began in March of 2020, and since that time, we've made tremendous progress in terms of serving the global autistic population through online meetings, advocacy, research, education, book publishing, and the fostering of connection amongst those navigating similar challenges. In more recent years, I've been personally involved as a research co-author partner to University College London, where myself and my fellow investigators have analyzed a large dataset of survey responses from autistic adults who self-reported about their own experiences with psychedelics in naturalistic (non-clinical) contexts. Our first research paper is scheduled to complete the peer review process to then be published as an open access publication by the end of 2023. And a second, followup investigation — involving a language analysis of the text fields completed during this same initial survey — is also underway, with a likely publish in 2024. Working with the UCL researchers has been an absolute honor. And our findings are sure to serve as a critical foundation upon which future clinical research will be built. In the meantime, Oregon and Colorado are slowly opening up for legal psilocybin access, and Australia is likewise preparing for its historic expansion of access by way of rescheduling MDMA (for the treatment of PTSD) as well as psilocybin (for treatment-resistant depression). With access to psychedelics rapidly expanding worldwide, the APC's present aim is to continue to amplify the voices of those who've benefitted from these medicines while also continuing to provide practical, evidence-based education to anyone who can stand to benefit. Thus, the intention of this book is to equip everyone with a sufficient level of context and background info so that we can more intelligently navigate autism, psychedelics, and the relevant intersections of the two. And while, yes, this book contains a lot of information, it's important to point out that we'll still need to complete a lot more research in order to help to ensure safety and efficacy for all....

Autistic Psychedelic Community

— About This Book —

This book is a followup to "Introduction To Psychedelic Autism", published in 2022. Within that introductory text, we explored anecdotal evidence and strived to answer the question "Why Might Psychedelics Matter to Autistics?" If you've not read that text, it's strongly encouraged that you do so, as the book provides essential foundational concepts as well as straight-forward explanations of how the APC operates as a global peer-support and mutual-aid network. Regardless of whether or not you have read through the previous book in this series — or any of the other literature published by Neurotopia Press (Autism On Acid, Autistic Psychedelic) — we nonetheless welcome you to read through this book so that you can more fully understand the full spread of evidence, principles, statistics, and approaches that are sure to inform the field of psychedelic autism care. Likewise, if you'd like to go beyond this book, we invite you to visit our website to learn more about our books, meetings, classes, consults, and more.

— Table of Contents —

AutisticPsychedelic.com

Psychedelic Neurodiversity
— A Non-Pathologized View of Autism Care —

What Is Autism?

DSM-Derived Definition

According to DSM-5, to meet diagnostic criteria for
autism, an individual must have persistent *"deficits"*
in EACH of the following three areas of social
communication and interaction....

Autistic Psychedelic Community

- **1.** *" Deficits in "* **social-emotional reciprocity**
  - *" Abnormal "* social approach
  - *" Failure of normal "* back-and-forth conversation
  - *" Reduced sharing of "* interests, emotions, or affect
  - *" Failures related to "* initiation or response to social interactions
- **2.** *"Deficits in"* **nonverbal communicative behaviors**
  - *" Total lack of "* facial expressions and nonverbal communication
  - *" Poorly integrated "* verbal and nonverbal communication
  - *" Abnormalities in "* eye contact and body language
  - *" Deficits in "* understanding and use of gestures

- **3.** *" Deficits in "* **developing, maintaining, and understanding relationships......**
  - *" Absence of "* interest toward peers
  - *" Difficulties in "* sharing imaginative play or making friends
  - *" Difficulties adjusting "* behavior to suit various social contexts

? Critical Questions for Contemplation **?**

*Might the terms in **RED** be a continuation of the pathologization model?*
What might the consequences of be of identifying with such language?
*What happens if we replace **RED TERMS** above with **"Differences In"**?*
What is gained & what is lost if we swap these terms? By whom?

AUTISTIC
PSYCHEDELIC

What Is Autism?

DSM-Derived Definition (continued)

Also, according to DSM-5, to meet diagnostic criteria for **autism**, an individual must have **at least two of the following four types of restricted, repetitive behaviors...**

What Is Autism?   (DSM-Derived Definition)

- **1. Stereotyped or repetitive motor movements or repetitive use of objects or speech, such as:**
  - ○ *Lining up toys or flipping objects*
  - ○ *Simple motor stereotypes* — repetitive movements or actions such as hand flapping, rocking, spinning (self-advocates' term: "stim")
  - ○ *Idiosyncratic phrases* — repetition of same phrases or words, the use of language in a rigid or inflexible way, or using words or phrases in atypical ways not understood by others.
  - ○ *Echolalia* — a term referring to a tendency to verbally repeat — either immediately or eventually — heard words or phrases in an effort to communicate or enhance language processing.

What Is Autism?

- **2. Insistence on sameness, inflexible adherence to routines, or ritualized patterns of verbal/nonverbal behaviors.**

  Examples of this include...

  - *Greeting rituals*, such as saying "hello" in a specific way or shaking hands in a specific way or consistently repeating phrases/actions
  - *Rigid thinking patterns*, including difficulties adapting to change or considering multiple perspectives, or a need for routines or sameness, or difficulties with abstract or open-ended concepts
  - *Difficulties with transitions*, including difficulties adapting to a new situation, and difficulties with flexibility and adaptability
  - *Needing to take same route or eat same food every day*

What Is Autism?

- **3. Highly restricted, fixated interests that are *"abnormal"* in intensity or focus:**

  Examples of this include...

  - *Excessively circumscribed or perseverative interests*
  - *Strong attachment to or preoccupation with unusual objects*

- **4. Hyper- or hyporeactivity to sensory input or unusual interest in sensory aspects of the environment:**

  - *Apparent indifference to pain/temperature*
  - *Adverse response to specific sounds or textures*
  - *Excessive smelling or touching of objects*
  - *Visual fascination with lights or movement*

The Pathology Paradigm

The Pathology Paradigm is a perspective that views **autism** as a disease or deficit that needs to be cured or eliminated.

Pathology Paradigm

The Pathology Paradigm has been traditionally dominant in the field of autism research and treatment, and it has often led to a focus on "negative" aspects of autism and an emphasis on reducing or eliminating autistic traits.

Some of the ways in which **The Pathology Paradigm** can impact the self-perception and the mental well-being of an autistic individual include...

Pathology Paradigm

(Impact of Pathology Paradigm)

- **Stigmatization and misunderstanding**
  - Many autistic individuals report feeling stigmatized and misunderstood because of the way that autism is often portrayed.
- **Marginalization**
  - "Fixing" or "normalizing" autistic individuals — instead of choosing to support unique strengths and needs — re-enforces otherness.
- **Limited support and accommodations**
  - The emphasis on trying to eliminate autistic traits can lead to a lack of support and accommodations for autistic differences. Without compassionate spaces to accommodate differences, certain forms of inalterable behavior have no place to exist.

Pathology vs Diversity

(Impact of Pathology Paradigm)

The Pathology Paradigm is highlighted here for the sake of contemplating the ways in which choices in language and perspective potentially impact the wellbeing of autistic individuals.

In response to the potential harms of **The Pathology Paradigm,** modern advocates often promote **The Neurodiversity Paradigm,** a perspective that views autism and other neurodevelopmental differences as natural forms of human diversity rather than pathologized disorders.

Neurodiversity Paradigm

In 2014, autistic PhD scholar Dr. Nick Walker (who also co-authored the MAPS MDMA social anxiety clinical trial for autistic adults) wrote the following updated definition of autism. In the words of Dr. Walker, this definition was made in an effort to discuss autism in a way that is...

1.) consistent with current evidence;

2.) not based in the pathology paradigm;

3.) concise, simple, and accessible;

4.) formal enough for professional and academic use.

ND Paradigm Definition of ASD

"Autism is a genetically-based human neurological variant. The complex set of interrelated characteristics that distinguish autistic neurology from non-autistic neurology is not yet fully understood, but current evidence indicates that the central distinction is that autistic brains are characterized by particularly high levels of synaptic connectivity and responsiveness. This tends to make the autistic individual's subjective experience more intense and chaotic than that of non-autistic individuals: on both the sensorimotor and cognitive levels, the autistic mind tends to register more information, and the impact of each bit of information tends to be both stronger and less predictable."

Source: Neuroqueer Heresies: Notes on the Neurodiversity Paradigm, Autistic Empowerment, and Postnormal Possibilities by Dr. Nick Walker

Pathology vs Diversity
(Comparative Criticism and Context)

BUT ALL OF THIS IS NOT SO SIMPLE AS A RED "X" AND A SMILEY FACE !
Just like the The Pathology Paradigm, The Neurodiversity Paradigm
has also been the subject of criticism for a number of reasons.
Let's look at some critiques of The Neurodiversity Paradigm.

Critiques of ND Paradigm (Comparative Criticism and Context)

- **Downplays Difficulties/Challenges**
  - While it is important to recognize and celebrate diversity, it's also important to acknowledge that some individuals need additional support or accommodations in order to fully participate in society.
- **Justifies a Lack of Interventions or Support**
  - While it is important to respect the autonomy and agency of individuals with neurological differences, it's also important to ensure they have access to the resources and support.
- **Perpetuates Potentially Harmful Stereotypes**
  - If concepts like "superpowers" are emphasized too strongly, it could re-enforce unrealistic expectations for some individuals.

ASD Comorbidities & Populations

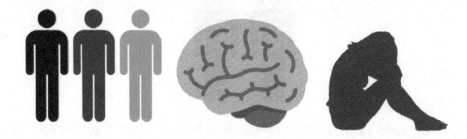

— Statistical Considerations for Professionals —

1 in Every 45 People in The United States is Autistic

Journal of Autism & Developmental Disorders. 2020
www.cdc.gov/ncbddd/autism/features/adults-living-with-autism-spectrum-disorder.html

Autistic Psychedelic Community

 ## ASD Comorbidities

- **Depression**: Up to 84% of autistics also experience comorbid depression
- **Anxiety:** Estimated 36% to 84% of individuals with ASD have comorbid anxiety
- **OCD**: Up to 20% of individuals with ASD also have comorbid OCD
- **Eating Disorder:** Up to 24% of individuals with ASD have E.D.comorbidity
- **Social Anxiety:** Up to 50% of individuals with ASD also have social anxiety
- **ADHD:** 30%-80% of individuals with ASD also have comorbid ADHD
  - **PTSD**: 32-45% of individuals with autism spectrum disorder (ASD) also have post-traumatic stress disorder (vs 5% in general pop)

- Source: Systemic Review Articles from Journal of Autism and Developmental Disorders, 2017-18

 ## ASD Intersectionality

- **Diagnosis Disparity**: Overall, black and Hispanic children are less likely than their white peers to have an autism diagnosis in the United States.
- **By Percentage:** White children are approximately 19% more likely than black children & 65% more likely than Hispanic children to be diagnosed with autism.
- **Accessibility**: Recent findings suggest that socioeconomic status doesn't fully explain the differences In prevalence across race and ethnicity, citing other factors such as average age of father and signs missed with ESL students..

- **Quote: "There is no biological reason for autism prevalence to differ across racial and ethnic groups"**-K.Zuckerman, Oregon H&SU

- Source: https://www.spectrumnews.org/news/race-class-contribute-disparities-autism-diagnoses/

Neurodiversity...
The concept that neurological differences — such as those seen in autism, ADHD, and dyslexia — should be celebrated/recognized as natural forms of human diversity

Neurodiversity Paradigm...
The perspective that recognizes and values the diversity of human brains and neurological function, rather than seeing it as a deficit that needs to be fixed or normalized

Neurodiversity Movement...
The social movement that advocates for the acceptance and inclusion of people with neurological differences, and challenges the dominant medical model of disability

Neurodivergent...
A person/brain that diverges from "typical" processing

Neurotypical...
A person/brain that falls within "typical" processing

Neurodiverse...
Referring to *a group or community* that includes individuals with a range of neurological differences and variations

Neurotype...
An individual's specific type or category of brain functioning

Cross-neurotype...
Interactions or communication between different neurotypes

Autistic Psychedelic Community

"An Updated View of Autism"

— Relevant Readings + Research —

Relevant Research/Readings

"AVOIDING ABLEIST LANGUAGE:

SUGGESTIONS FOR AUTISM RESEARCHERS"

Kristen Bottema-Beutel, PhD, Steven K. Kapp, PhD, Jessica Nina Lester, PhD, Noah J. Sasson, PhD, and Brittany Hand, PhD, OTR

Autism In Adulthood, 2020

Scan to
View Paper

Autistic Psychedelic Community

"AVOIDING ABLEIST LANGUAGE: SUGGESTIONS FOR AUTISM RESEARCHERS"

Paper Highlights

- Authors express that despite some improvements, ableist language (language that assumes disabled people are inferior) is still used in autism research, treatment, and general public discourse.

- Authors suggest the avoidance of using terms like "special interests" and "special needs," which may be perceived as patronizing.

- Authors suggest neutral language like "increased likelihood of autism" instead of medicalized/deficit language like "at risk for autism."

SOURCE: HTTPS://DOI.ORG/10.1089/AUT.2020.0014

Relevant Research/Readings

"NEUROTYPE-MATCHING, BUT NOT BEING AUTISTIC, INFLUENCES SELF & OBSERVER RATINGS OF INTERPERSONAL RAPPORT"

Catherine J. Crompton, Martha Sharp, Harriet Axbey, Sue Fletcher-Watson, Emma G. Flynn, and Danielle Ropar

Frontiers in Psychology, 2020

Scan to View Paper

 "NEUROTYPE-MATCHING, BUT NOT BEING AUTISTIC, INFLUENCES SELF & OBSERVER RATINGS OF INTERPERSONAL RAPPORT"

Study Methods

- *Two studies* were conducted to examine whether self- and observer-rated rapport varies depending on the match or mismatch in autism status within a pair.

- *In Study 1*, non-autistic pairs had higher *self-rated* rapport than mixed & autistic pairs, & autistic pairs had higher rapport than mixed pairs.

- *In Study 2*, mixed pairs were *rated significantly lower by others* on rapport than autistic and non-autistic pairs, and autistic pairs were rated more highly for rapport than non-autistic pairs.

SOURCE: HTTPS://FRONTIERSIN.ORG/ARTICLES/10.3389/FPSYG.2020.586171/FULL

 "NEUROTYPE-MATCHING, BUT NOT BEING AUTISTIC, INFLUENCES SELF & OBSERVER RATINGS OF INTERPERSONAL RAPPORT"

Key Takeaways...

- These findings suggest that <u>autistic people experience high interactional rapport when interacting with other autistic people</u>, and this is also detected by external observers.

- The data suggest that <u>autistic people possess a distinct mode of social interaction style</u>, rather than demonstrating social skills deficits.

- These findings have implications for psychological theories of autism and practical impact on educational and clinical practices

SOURCE: HTTPS://FRONTIERSIN.ORG/ARTICLES/10.3389/FPSYG.2020.586171/FULL

Autistic Psychedelic Community

"AUTISTIC SELF-ADVOCACY AND THE NEURODIVERSITY MOVEMENT: IMPLICATIONS FOR AUTISM EARLY INTERVENTION RESEARCH AND PRACTICE"

Kathy Leadbitter, Karen Leneh Buckle, Ceri Ellis, Martijn Dekker

Frontiers in Psychology, 2021

Scan to
View
Paper

 "AUTISTIC SELF-ADVOCACY & THE NEURODIVERSITY MOVEMENT: IMPLICATIONS FOR EARLY INTERVENTION RESEARCH PRACTICE"

Key Takeaways

- The emergence of the internet in the mid-1990s enabled autistic people to connect and share ideas, leading to the development of autistic culture, the autistic self-advocacy movement, and the neurodiversity movement

- The neurodiversity movement has had an impact on *some* areas of autism research and treatment, particularly those focused on adults.

  - Authors propose "intervention practices with greater emphasis on natural developmental processes, coping strategies, autonomy, and self-directed well-being.

SOURCE: HTTPS://WWW.FRONTIERSIN.ORG/ARTICLES/10.3389/FPSYG.2021.635690/FULL

Autistic Psychedelic Community

"AUTISM AND THE DOUBLE EMPATHY PROBLEM: IMPLICATIONS FOR DEVELOPMENT AND MENTAL HEALTH"

Peter Mitchell, Elizabeth Sheppard, and Sarah Cassidy

British Journal of Developmental Psychology, 2021

Scan to View Paper

 "AUTISM AND THE DOUBLE EMPATHY PROBLEM: IMPLICATIONS FOR DEVELOPMENT AND MENTAL HEALTH"

Article Highlights

- Authors propose that "The exclusion of autistic individuals from society may also prevent neurotypical individuals from learning from cross-neurotype social interactions, thus increasing divisions within society."

- The article in particular does an excellent job of bringing this discussion full circle in terms of considering neurotypical gains and losses as they might relate to autistic inclusion/disclusion.

  - Article also features some well-structured visual aids, and insights relevant to "do-no-harms-first" care approaches.

SOURCE: HTTPS://BPSPSYCHUB.ONLINELIBRARY.WILEY.COM/DOI/FULL/10.1111/BJDP.12350

"AUTISM AND THE DOUBLE EMPATHY PROBLEM: IMPLICATIONS FOR DEVELOPMENT AND MENTAL HEALTH"

Important Quote...

"We propose that how the behaviour of autistic people is perceived by neurotypical others (negatively), influences how they behave towards autistic people (unwelcoming), which is then perceived by autistic people (that they are not welcome), which then impacts on the behaviour of autistic people (perhaps wariness, mistrust, low self-esteem, lack of social ability due to lack of positive and rewarding social experience). This in turn will impact on how autistic people are perceived by neurotypical others (negatively), and so on."

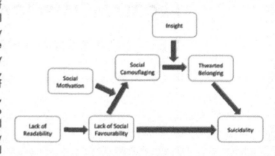

SOURCE: HTTPS://BPSPSYCHUB.ONLINELIBRARY.WILEY.COM/DOI/FULL/10.1111/BJDP.12350

"AUTISM AND THE DOUBLE EMPATHY PROBLEM: IMPLICATIONS FOR DEVELOPMENT AND MENTAL HEALTH"

Important Quote...

"[The medical model] locates the problems of autism within the individual, with the assumption that the individual must be treated to effect change in order to make the problem go away. Common approaches have been to apply behaviour techniques, to administer medication, implementing programs of therapy and offering dedicated teaching on how to understand other people's minds. Such interventions are likely to cause autistic people to feel they are defective and that they need to change in order to fit into society. Being subjected to these interventions could lead to a sense of thwarted belonging ('If you can't change then you are not welcome!') and, associated with that, a desire to camouflage autistic features. If so, ironically, and despite all good intentions, these interventions might put the individual at risk of mental health issues and even increased risk of suicide."

SOURCE: HTTPS://BPSPSYCHUB.ONLINELIBRARY.WILEY.COM/DOI/FULL/10.1111/BJDP.12350

Autistic Psychedelic Community

Psychedelic Substance Profiles

— Helpful Categories + Labels —

 **PSYCHEDELIC**

"Psychedelic" is a term defined in so many ways....

The term was first coined in 1957 by British psychiatrist
Humphry Osmond, who combined the Greek words...

ψυχή **"psyche"**
('soul, mind')

+

δηλοῦν **"deloun"**
('to manifest', 'to reveal', 'to make plain or evident')

Autistic Psychedelic Community

 ## PSYCHEDELIC

— *Alternate Definitions* —

"(of a drug) causing effects on the mind, such as feelings of deep understanding or unusually strong experiences of color, sound, taste, and touch :."

- Cambridge English Dictionary

 ## PSYCHEDELIC

— *Alternate Definitions* —

"Psychedelics (serotonergic hallucinogens) are powerful psychoactive substances that alter perception and mood and affect numerous cognitive processes. They are generally considered physiologically safe and do not lead to dependence or addiction."

- Pharmacologist David E. Nichols, PhD

Psychedelic Substance Profiles

— Helpful Categories + Labels —

 **ENTACTO**-GENS

"Entactogen" is a term used to describe **MDMA** — and sometimes, also, *psilocybin*/**LSD.**

"En-Tact-O-Gen" composed of the Greek roots "en" + "gen" (to generate within) + Latin "tactus" meaning "touch". Hence, entactogens are **exogenous substances that allow or promote a touching within or reaching inside** to retrieve memories/somatic insight.

Autistic Psychedelic Community

EMPATHO-GENS

"Empathogen" is a term that also describes MDMA — and sometimes, also, psilocybin/LSD or other compounds like kava, cacao, cannabis, etc.

Empathogen are known to increase *implicit* & *explicit* empathy scores and/or social bonding. MDMA is a classic example. MDMA experiences often give users a heightened sense of connection and/or an increased willingness to express or experience shared emotions.

ENTHEO-GENS

"Entheogens" are psychoactive substances used in a religious, spiritual, or shamanic context to induce a transformative experience.

The term "entheogen" is derived from the Greek words "entheos" (full of the divine) and "gen" (generate). Some people use term to describe any substance used for spiritual or religious purposes; others reserve term for describing substances known to produce a specifically transformative or general "mystical" or "expansive" experience.

Autistic Psychedelic Community

DISSOCIATIVES

"DISSOCIATIVE" is a term that describes *ketamine* and other substances known to produce a sense of detachment from one's surroundings and body.

It's worth noting that effects of such drugs can vary widely from person to person, and that the classification of these drugs into specific categories is somewhat arbitrary and depends on dose and intent. Ketamine is a great example of this in that, yes, it has dissociative effects, but it's pharmacological action is also known to induce anti-depressant outcomes...

Psychedelic Substance Overview

— Substance-Specific Profiles —

PSILOCYBIN

Psilocybin is a partial serotonergic agonist compound found in certain species of mushrooms (can also be synthesized)

- **Other Names:** "Magic Mushrooms", "Los Niños Santos"

- **Therapeutic Potential**: Therapeutic potential in the treatment of a variety of conditions, including depression, anxiety, and addiction.

- **Mechanism of Action:** Not fully understood, but believed to work by binding to serotonin receptors, leading to changes in brain activity

  - **Origin of Compound**: Found naturally in mushroom species, including Psilocybe cubensis, Psilocybe semilanceata, and Psilocybe cyanescens.

PSILOCYBIN

- **Typical Dose Amounts:**
  - Microdose:
    - 100-250 milligrams of dry weight fruiting body
    - 1-2 milligrams of isolated, synthetic psilocybin compound
  - Macrodose:
    - 1-5 grams of dry weight fruiting body (5g is max/session in Oregon)
    - 10-30 milligrams of isolated, synthetic psilocybin compound

- **Dosing Logic:** Often dosed mg/kg in clinical and medical contexts

- **Preparation:** Can be consumed raw, as a tea, or with preparatory "teks"

  - **Potential Side Effects:** Nausea, vomiting, and changes in perception, mood, "bad trips", may trigger psychosis/schizophrenia

Autistic Psychedelic Community

LSD

LSD (lysergic acid diethylamide) is a partial serotonergic agonist known for altering perception and emotional processing.

- **Other Names:** "L", "LSD", "Acid",

- **Therapeutic Potential**: Similar to psilocybin, with main differentiator being that LSD has longer duration of acute drug effect (6-10hrs) vs. psilo (4-6hrs)

- **Mechanism of Action:** Not fully understood, but believed to work by binding to several serotonin receptors *as well as* certain dopamine receptors

  - **Origin of Compound**: Synthesized from a variety of chemicals, including ergotamine, which is found in the ergot fungus that grows on grains

LSD

- **Typical Dose Amounts:**
  - Microdose:
    - 1-15 micrograms
    - *Recent study: "13 micrograms may be ideal subperceptive dose")*
  - Macrodose:
    - 100-700 micrograms
    - *Largest dose consumed by a human: 55mg (550x typical dose)*

- **Dosing Logic:** No evidence thus far that body weight is a factor in dosing

- **Preparation:** Consumed orally via liquid drops or "blotter" doses

  - **Potential Side Effects:** Nausea, vomiting, and changes in perception, mood, "bad trips", may trigger psychosis/schizophrenia

MDMA

MDMA *an indirect monoaminergic agonist, stimulating the release and inhibiting reuptake of serotonin (5-HT) and, to a lesser extent, other neurotransmitters.*

- **Other Names:** "Ecstasy" or "Molly", often adulterated when sold underground
- **Therapeutic Potential**: Treating post-traumatic stress disorder (PTSD) and other anxiety disorders, addiction, etc. by reducing fear/stress response
- **Mechanism of Action:** Not fully understood, but evidence supports that MDMA increases presence of serotonin, dopamine, oxytocin, and norepinephrine — neurotransmitters involved in mood regulation/social-emotional processing
  - **Origin of Compound**: Synthesized from a variety of chemicals, including safrole, which is found in the sassafras plant.

MDMA

- **Typical Dose:** Typically administered in the range of 75-125 mg, sometimes followed by booster doses to sustain drug effect and prolong therapeutic window. Microdosing MDMA is conventionally inadvisable.

- **Dosing Logic:** Varies, but typically 1-1.5 mg/kg of body weight.

- **Dosing Logic Example:** Someone who weighs 70 kg (154 lbs) would typically take a dose of 70-105 mg of MDMA for a moderate effect.
  - **Potential Side Effects:**
    - Increased heart rate and blood pressure
    - Dehydration, dry mouth
    - Chronic use can lead to challenges with memory recall

Autistic Psychedelic Community

KETAMINE

Ketamine is a dissociative anesthetic substance that can be utilized in conjunction with assistive therapy protocols to potentially address a range of general health issues

- **Other Names:** "K"
- **Therapeutic Potential:** Ketamine-assisted therapy has been reported effective in reducing depression, anxiety, and chronic pain, with other reported benefits such as improving sleep or reducing suicidal thoughts.
- **Mechanism of Action:**
  - There are many potential targets. One such is the way in which Ketamine disrupts normal functioning of the glutamate, a neurotransmitter involved in cognition, memory, and emotion.

AYAHUASCA

Ayahuasca is a psychoactive brew made from Banisteriopsis caapi vine and the leaves of Psychotria viridis plant

- **Other Names:** "Aya", "Grandmother"

- **Preparation Methods:** Boiling the stems and leaves of the Banisteriopsis caapi vine and the leaves of the Psychotria viridis plant.

- **Origin of Compound:** Contains a mixture of compounds, including the psychoactive alkaloids dimethyltryptamine (DMT) and harmine.

  - **Therapeutic Potential:** Treatment of a variety of conditions, including depression, anxiety, and addiction — less often studied in research as per limitations of IP-focused funding in drug development industries

  ## DMT / 5-MEO-DMT

DMT and *5-MeO-DMT* are powerful visionary compounds found in a variety of plants and animals (can also be synthesized)

It's worth noting that DMT and 5-MeO-DMT are both receiving renewed interest from modern research because of (1) fast-onset/short-lasting effects and (2) because these substances have shown to very reliably induce experiences rated "high" in terms of ratings of "mysticality". While there is certainly room to explore this frontier, the general comprehension of these molecules and their utility is presently nascent, with some of the first brain imaging data sets just now becoming available within the past year.

"A Look Back At Relevant Research"
— *Pre-Prohibition Era Findings* —

Autistic Psychedelic Community

"LSD & UML TREATMENT OF HOSPITALIZED DISTURBED CHILDREN"

Liuretta Bender, hi, D., Gloria Faretra, M.D., and Leonard

Cobrinik. Ph.D.

Recent Advances in Biological Psychiatry, 1963

Scan to View Paper

 "LSD & UML TREATMENT OF HOSPITALIZED DISTURBED CHILDREN"

Study Design

- Study looked at effects of LSD & UML on autistic children (6-12 years)
- Children had varying degrees of support needs / language capacity
- Many were unresponsive to environment, disorganized sleeping habits
- Most individuals had low scores on standard psychological tests
- Subjects were given LSD or UML (another ergot-derived compound) in treatment sessions, with daily LSD dosing increasing from 60 micrograms up to 150 micrograms

SOURCE: HTTPS://NEURODIVERSITY.COM/LIBRARY_BENDER_1963.HTML

Autistic Psychedelic Community

 "LSD & UML TREATMENT OF HOSPITALIZED DISTURBED CHILDREN"

Study Outcomes

- LSD/UML caused changes in responsiveness to environment, including increased alertness, awareness, interest in others, facial expression.

- Both LSD and UML had observed effects on children's behavior and psychological functioning

- While not categorized as "serious" adverse effects, some participants experienced intense anxiety, confusion, tantrum-like behaviors

SOURCE: HTTPS://NEURODIVERSITY.COM/LIBRARY_BENDER_1963.HTML

 "LSD & UML TREATMENT OF HOSPITALIZED DISTURBED CHILDREN"

Study Limitations

- Study raises serious ethical issues regarding informed consent

- Study took place many decades ago with different diagnostic criteria

- Study involved dosing amounts and regularity rarely ever otherwise studied or practiced even amidst expansion of anectodal reporting

- Study is limited to assessments provided by observants, and included a lack of more "objective" metrics that would be more commonly applied in modern research (e.g., brain imaging, advanced bloodwork, etc.)

SOURCE: HTTPS://NEURODIVERSITY.COM/LIBRARY_BENDER_1963.HTML

Autistic Psychedelic Community

"MODIFICATION OF AUTISTIC BEHAVIOR WITH LSD-25"

J.Q. Simmons 3rd, S.J. Leiken, O.I. Lovaas,

B. Schaeffer, B. Perloff

Archives of General Psychiatry, 1966

Scan to View Paper

"MODIFICATION OF AUTISTIC BEHAVIOR WITH LSD-25"

Study Design

- The study consisted of two parts. In both parts, subjects were given either an inert placebo or 50 micrograms of LSD in pill form.

- Study participants were twins, 5 years old, with "failure to make use of objects appropriately and subsequent failure to develop speech."

- Tests consisted of social/play-based situations "pat-a-cake", "peek-a-boo", etc. as well as open play with no observers present in the room.

- Behaviors were recorded during control/experimental sessions

SOURCE: HTTP://NEURODIVERSITY.COM/LIBRARY_SIMMONS_1966.PDF

AutisticPsychedelic.com

"MODIFICATION OF AUTISTIC BEHAVIOR WITH LSD-25"

Study Outcomes

- Subjects showed increase in social behaviors, including increased eye-to-face contact increased responsiveness to adults, and decrease in self-stimulatory behavior

- Subjects also displayed increased smiling and laughing behavior, which may indicate change in mood/perception of external stimuli

- Limitation/context: only 2 subjects observed; both had relatively unchanging behavior beyond acute drug window

SOURCE: HTTP://NEURODIVERSITY.COM/LIBRARY_SIMMONS_1966.PDF

Relevant Research/Readings

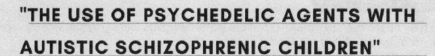

"THE USE OF PSYCHEDELIC AGENTS WITH AUTISTIC SCHIZOPHRENIC CHILDREN"

Robert E. Mogar & Robert W. Aldrich

The Psychedelic Review, 1969

Scan to View Paper

Autistic Psychedelic Community

"THE USE OF PSYCHEDELIC AGENTS WITH AUTISTIC SCHIZOPHRENIC CHILDREN"

Article Highlights

- This review summarizes multiple pre-prohibition-era studies examining potential applications of psilocybin, LSD & UML

- Seven independent studies were reviewed a total of 91 austistic schizophrenic children who received psychedelic compounds

- Large majority of children treated in studies were 6-10 years of age and were completely refractory to all other forms of treatment

"THE USE OF PSYCHEDELIC AGENTS WITH AUTISTIC SCHIZOPHRENIC CHILDREN"

Article Highlights

- A variety of psychedelic agents, dosage levels, frequency of administrations, and treatment schedules were employed.

- The most effective results were observed with 100+ microgram doses of LSD-25 given either **daily or weekly** (!) over extended periods of time.

- Differences in patient attributes, treatment technique, research design, and other non-drug factors seemed to affect the frequency and stability of favorable outcomes.

Autistic Psychedelic Community

"THE USE OF PSYCHEDELIC AGENTS WITH AUTISTIC SCHIZOPHRENIC CHILDREN"

Study Outcomes

- The most consistent effects reported in these studies included...
  - Improved speech behavior in otherwise mute children
  - Increased emotional responsiveness to other children and adults
  - Elevation in positive mood including frequent laughter
  - Decreases in compulsive ritualistic behavior

"THE USE OF PSYCHEDELIC AGENTS WITH AUTISTIC SCHIZOPHRENIC CHILDREN"

Examiner Quotes

"The vocabularies of several of the children increased after LSD or UML; several seemed to be attempting to form words or watched adults carefully as they spoke; many seemed to comprehend speech for the first time or were able to communicate their needs... Very few of these changes in communication had been noted previously in such a large number of children, and at such a relatively rapid rate..."

"THE USE OF PSYCHEDELIC AGENTS WITH AUTISTIC SCHIZOPHRENIC CHILDREN"

Examiner Quotes

"They appeared flushed, bright eyed, and unusually interested in the environment... They participated with increasing eagerness in motility play with adults and other children..."

"They seek positive contacts with adults, approaching them with face uplifted and bright eyes, and responding to fondling, affection, etc..."

SOURCE: HTTPS://BIBLIOGRAPHY.MAPS.ORG/RESOURCE/4639

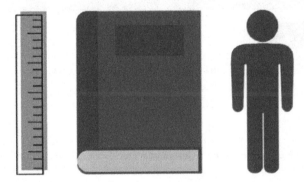

"A Look Back At Relevant Research"
— Modern "Renaissance" Era Findings —

Relevant Research/Readings

"EFFECTS OF SEROTONIN 2A/1A RECEPTOR STIMULATION ON SOCIAL EXCLUSION PROCESSING"

Preller et al, 2015

Proceedings of the National Academy of Sciences

Scan to View Paper

 "EFFECTS OF SEROTONIN 2A/1A RECEPTOR STIMULATION ON SOCIAL EXCLUSION PROCESSING"

Study Design

- This study looked at how psilocybin might change the way the brain responds to social rejection using a virtual game of pass-the-ball.
- The study included 21 "typically developing" volunteers who took psilocybin or a placebo then completed tasks in a brain scanner.
- During study, those who took psilocybin reported feeling less rejected and had less activity in regions of brain involved in negative states associated with social rejection.

HTTPS://RESEARCHGATE.NET/PUBLICATION/301483927_EFFECTS_OF_SEROTONIN_2A1A
_RECEPTOR_STIMULATION_ON_SOCIAL_EXCLUSION_PROCESSING

Autistic Psychedelic Community

"EFFECTS OF SEROTONIN 2A/1A RECEPTOR STIMULATION ON SOCIAL EXCLUSION PROCESSING"

Study Implications

- These findings suggest that psilocybin might be helpful for treating certain mental health conditions that involve feeling rejected

- Findings also offer mechanistic understanding of how psilocybin and 2A receptors might influence or modulate rejection response

- Findings may be of particular interest to autistic individuals as they may be more prone to needing to overcome or challenge conditioned beliefs of rejection in order to rehabilitate social skills.

HTTPS://RESEARCHGATE.NET/PUBLICATION/301483927_EFFECTS_OF_SEROTONIN_2A1A
_RECEPTOR_STIMULATION_ON_SOCIAL_EXCLUSION_PROCESSING

Relevant Research/Readings

LSD ACUTELY IMPAIRS FEAR RECOGNITION & ENHANCES EMOTIONAL EMPATHY & SOCIALITY

Dolder, et al, 2016

Nature – Neuropsychopharmacology

Scan to View Paper

AutisticPsychedelic.com

"LSD ACUTELY IMPAIRS FEAR RECOGNITION & ENHANCES EMOTIONAL EMPATHY & SOCIALITY"

Study Design

- Study aimed to examine effects of LSD on emotions and social behavior in healthy adults
- Two studies were conducted:
  - Study 1: 100 micrograms of LSD given to 24 healthy subjects
  - Study 2: 200 micrograms of LSD given to 16 healthy subjects
  - Washout period of at least 7 days was implemented

SOURCE: HTTPS://WWW.NATURE.COM/ARTICLES/NPP201682

"LSD ACUTELY IMPAIRS FEAR RECOGNITION & ENHANCES EMOTIONAL EMPATHY & SOCIALITY"

Study Demographic

- **Participants:** 40 "healthy adults" recruited
  - **Ages:** 25 - 60 years of age
  - **Prior Use of Psychedelics:** 29 out of 40 reported no prior use
  - **Inclusions:** "healthy adults" refers to those who (1) do not have a 1st-degree relatives with major psychiatric disorder and (2) are not on contraindicated meds

SOURCE: HTTPS://WWW.NATURE.COM/ARTICLES/NPP201682

"LSD ACUTELY IMPAIRS FEAR RECOGNITION & ENHANCES EMOTIONAL EMPATHY & SOCIALITY"

Study Procedure

- **Assessment:** at 5 hrs, then 7 hrs after dosing, following exams given:
  - **Facial Emotion Recognition Task (FERT):** participants sequentially look at faces (each rated for emotionality) and participants then indicating the certainty of what they observed
  - **Multifaceted Empathy Test (MET):** participants look at different images to "infer the mental state of subject and indicate the correct mental state from list of four responses."

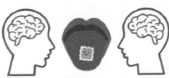

SOURCE: HTTPS://WWW.NATURE.COM/ARTICLES/NPP201682

"LSD ACUTELY IMPAIRS FEAR RECOGNITION & ENHANCES EMOTIONAL EMPATHY & SOCIALITY" (EXAMPLE OF FERT TEST)

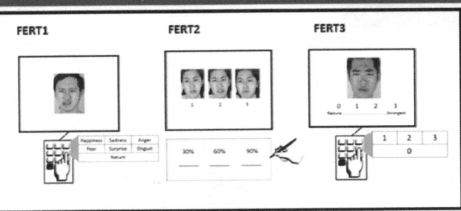

SOURCE: RESEARCHGATE.NET/FIGURE/THE-FACIAL-EMOTION-RECOGNITION-TASK-FERT_FIG1_330154394

"LSD ACUTELY IMPAIRS FEAR RECOGNITION & ENHANCES EMOTIONAL EMPATHY & SOCIALITY" (EXAMPLE OF FERT TEST)

Study Results

Figure 1

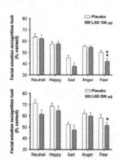

Lysergic acid diethylamide (LSD) impaired fear recognition on the Face Emotion Recognition Task. LSD also impaired the decoding of sad faces (significant main effect of drug), but the effects did not reach statistical significance in the individual dose groups. The data are expressed as mean±SEM in 22 and 16 subjects in the 100 and 200 µg LSD dose groups,

Figure 2

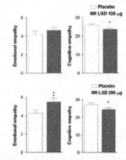

Lysergic acid diethylamide (LSD) increased emotional empathy and decreased cognitive empathy on the Multifaceted Empathy Test. The data are expressed as mean±SEM in 22 and 16 subjects in the 100 and 200µg LSD dose groups, respectively. *$p<0.05$, **$p<0.01$, significant difference from placebo.

"LSD ACUTELY IMPAIRS FEAR RECOGNITION & ENHANCES EMOTIONAL EMPATHY & SOCIALITY"

Relevance+Context

- Study illuminates potential use of LSD (or other serotonergic compounds) to induce modulations of perception and/or processing of visual or emotional facial information

- Worth noting: this study involved dose amounts that are more typically associated with visionary or "hallucinogenic" experiences

- Although this study was not autism-focused, it's interesting to consider what lower-dose study might look like if study comparing outcomes of autistic vs. non-autistic groups

SOURCE: HTTPS://WWW.NATURE.COM/ARTICLES/NPP201682

Autistic Psychedelic Community

PSILOCYBIN & MDMA REDUCE COSTLY PUNISHMENT IN THE ULTIMATUM GAME

Gabay et al, Scientific Reports, 2018

Scan to View Paper

PSILOCYBIN & MDMA REDUCE COSTLY PUNISHMENT IN THE ULTIMATUM GAME

Study At A Glance

- Two studies were conducted to investigate the effects of MDMA and psilocybin on social decision-making using the Ultimatum Game (UG) paradigm.

- In the UG, participants decide whether to reject or accept an offer made by another person or a random, computer-generated offer...

- Both psilocybin and MDMA reduced rejection of "unfair offers" in the UG. The reduction in rejection rate specifically with MDMA was associated with increased pro-sociality.

SOURCE: HTTPS://DOI.ORG/10.1038/S41598-018-26656-2

Autistic Psychedelic Community

REDUCTION IN SOCIAL ANXIETY AFTER MDMA-ASSISTED PSYCHOTHERAPY WITH AUTISTIC ADULTS: A RANDOMIZED, DOUBLE-BLIND, PLACEBO-CONTROLLED PILOT STUDY

Scan to View Paper

Danforth et al, Psychopharmacology, 2018

REDUCTION IN SOCIAL ANXIETY AFTER MDMA-ASSISTED PSYCHOTHERAPY WITH AUTISTIC ADULTS: A RANDOMIZED, DOUBLE-BLIND, PLACEBO-CONTROLLED PILOT STUDY

Study Design

- Study explored MDMA-assisted therapy as treatment for social anxiety in autistic adults
- 12 subjects were divided into two groups:
  - One group of 8 subjects received MDMA
  - One group of 4 subjects received a placebo
- Primary outcome measure was change in scores on Leibowitz Social Anxiety Scale (LSAS), assessing comparison of baseline to one month after the second experimental session

SOURCE: HTTPS://DOI.ORG/10.1007/S00213-018-5010-9

REDUCTION IN SOCIAL ANXIETY AFTER MDMA-ASSISTED PSYCHOTHERAPY WITH AUTISTIC ADULTS: A RANDOMIZED, DOUBLE-BLIND, PLACEBO-CONTROLLED PILOT STUDY

Study Design

- The study used a placebo-controlled, double-blind design...
  - 8 participants received MDMA (75 to 125 mg per session)
  - 4 participants received a inactive placebo during both sessions
- All participants received three preparatory 60-90 min non-drug prep sessions before AND after each experimental dosing session (in which placebo or blind was used)
- Total treatment: nine prep/integration sessions + two 8-hour dosing sessions

SOURCE: HTTPS://DOI.ORG/10.1007/S00213-018-5010-9

REDUCTION IN SOCIAL ANXIETY AFTER MDMA-ASSISTED PSYCHOTHERAPY WITH AUTISTIC ADULTS: A RANDOMIZED, DOUBLE-BLIND, PLACEBO-CONTROLLED PILOT STUDY

Study Outcomes

- Results showed significant improvement in LSAS scores for MDMA vs placebo group
- Study supports MDMA-assisted therapy in terms of providing "rapid & durable improvement" in social anxiety symptoms in autistic adults

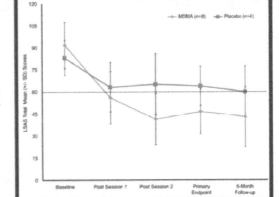

Fig. 2

SOURCE: HTTPS://DOI.ORG/10.1007/S00213-018-5010-9

Autistic Psychedelic Community

"SUB-ACUTE EFFECTS OF PSILOCYBIN ON EMPATHY, CREATIVE THINKING, AND SUBJECTIVE WELL-BEING"

Mason et al, Biological Psychiatry, 2019

Scan to View Paper

 "SUB-ACUTE EFFECTS OF PSILOCYBIN ON EMPATHY, CREATIVE THINKING & SUBJECTIVE WELL-BEING"

Study Design

- Participants completed tests of creative thinking, empathy, and well-being before and after taking psilocybin truffles at a retreat in Netherlands

- Participants received doses of psilocybin-containing truffles — the natural form that mushrooms exist as prior to forming a fruiting body — which are also legal to purchase and consume from smart shops and other vendors in NL

SOURCE: HTTPS://DOI.ORG/10.1080/02791072.2019.1580804

"SUB-ACUTE EFFECTS OF PSILOCYBIN ON EMPATHY, CREATIVE THINKING & SUBJECTIVE WELL-BEING"

Retreat Context

- After taking psilo in morning, participants were instructed to stay on retreat premises, and were able to do whatever they pleased, as long as they did not disturb other participants or leave the grounds.

- Facilitators provided music, tools to draw and/or write, and food. In the evening, all participants and facilitators came back together as a group.

- The next morning, all participants had breakfast together, followed by a closing sharing circle, after which surveys were then taken

SOURCE: HTTPS://DOI.ORG/10.1080/02791072.2019.1580804

"SUB-ACUTE EFFECTS OF PSILOCYBIN ON EMPATHY, CREATIVE THINKING & SUBJECTIVE WELL-BEING"

Study Outcomes

- Psilocybin retreat goers reported enhanced divergent thinking and emotional empathy the morning after use and that these enhancements persisted through until the 7-day followup

- Study also found psilocybin increased well-being and that changes in self-rated implicit/explicit emotional empathy were correlated with changes in well-being

- These findings suggest that a single administration of psilocybin in a social setting may enhance creative thinking, empathy, and well-being

SOURCE: HTTPS://DOI.ORG/10.1080/02791072.2019.1580804

Autistic Psychedelic Community

"PSILOCYBIN RESCUES SOCIABILITY DEFICITS IN AN ANIMAL MODEL OF AUTISM"

Mollinedo-Gajate et al, Frontiers in Pharmacology, 2021

"PSILOCYBIN RESCUES SOCIABILITY DEFICITS IN AN ANIMAL MODEL OF AUTISM"

Study Design

- Researchers used mice exposed to valproic acid (VPA) in utero — a modeling approach that has been used to study ASD-like behavior — in order to investigate the potential of psilocybin to improve social behavior in individuals with ASD.

- Mice exposed to VPA in utero showed impaired social behavior (as measured by duration of nose touches and other metrics) compared to control mice

- Psilocybin improved social behavior in both the control mice group and the VPA group, but the effect change was much more significant in VPA group

SOURCE: HTTPS://DOI.ORG/10.1101/2020.09.09.289348

Autistic Psychedelic Community

Currently Legal Psychedelic Care

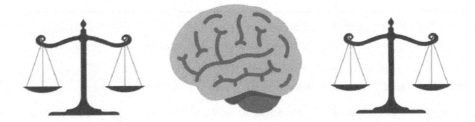

— Substance-Free Access to Psychedelic States—

Meditation & Mindfulness

Meditation & Mindfulness *practices involve focusing one's attention on present moment & sensations, without judgment.*

- Helps autistics develop awareness of their thoughts, feelings, and sensations, which can improve their ability to regulate their emotions and behaviors

- Helps develop greater clarity and focus, which can improve autistic individual's ability to learn and retain information

- Contemplative practices provide enhanced perspective of others and the ability to express one's thoughts and feelings in a clear and concise manner

    - Evidence suggests such practices can improve sleep and be effective in managing physical health conditions such as chronic pain or GI issues

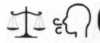 ## Holotropic Breathwork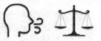

***Holotropic Breathwork** involves use of accelerated breathing and music to facilitate an altered state of consciousness..*

- Developed by psychiatrist Stanislav Grof and based on belief that unconscious mind holds key to understanding and healing psychological and physical issues

- May be helpful to individuals with ASD as it can help to release repressed emotions and memories that may be contributing to trait presentations

- May also help individuals manage stress and anxiety, as it can provide a safe and supportive environment for exploring and releasing difficult emotions

- Typically conducted in a group setting, which may be beneficial for individuals with ASD who may struggle with social interactions

 ## Sensory Deprivation Tanks

***Sensory Deprivation Tanks** are specially designed to create a calming environment that is free of sensory input*

- S.D. tanks are typically filled with solution of body-temperature-heated water and Epsom salt, which allows the body to float effortlessly

- Tanks can induce a psychedelic state by removing external stimuli, which can allow the mind to enter into a state of altered consciousness

- Provide a sense of relaxation and reduced anxiety, which can be beneficial for individuals who may struggle with sensory processing

- Sessions typically last 45 minutes to 90 minutes, allowing for routine accessibility that can support other therapies and modalities

 ## Yoga + Somatic Practices

Yoga and Somatic Practices *involve using the body to explore and understand one's emotions and internal experiences.*

- Somatic practices and yoga can be modified to meet needs and abilities of individuals with ASD, making them suitable for a range of individuals

- Can be practiced in variety of settings, including at home, in a class, or in group setting, making them accessible to individuals of all ages/abilities

- Can be paired with post-session practices such as guided meditations or reflection exercises to further enhance mindfulness and awareness

- Generally very accessible, with most cities having at least a few dedicated facilities offering classes and trainings

History of Legality + Scheduling

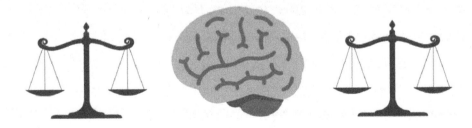

— Timelines + Context for Each Compound —

Autistic Psychedelic Community

PSILOCYBIN LEGALITY

Psilocybin is a federally illegal Schedule I substance in USA;
(various states/nations/regions have different access abroad)

- **For Millenia:** Used in indigenous/lineage traditions
- **1958:** Synthesized by Swiss chemist Albert Hofmann, who also synthesized LSD.
- **1960s:** Remained legal and studied for potential therapeutic benefits, particularly in the treatment of alcoholism and neurosis — also autism.
- **1970:** Drug Act classified psilocybin as Schedule I controlled substance in US
- **Today:** Psilocybin has a patchwork of legal access around the world...
  Legal medicine in US/Canada for "compassionate care" access.
  More about current/future access in Session III of this course.

LSD LEGALITY

LSD is a federally illegal Schedule I substance in USA with no
immediately predictable legalization path w/o FDA approval

- **1938:** LSD first synthesized by Swiss chemist Albert Hofmann.
- **1950s + 1960s:** LSD studied for its potential therapeutic benefits, particularly in the treatment of alcoholism and other mental health conditions.
- **1970:** LSD classified as a Schedule I controlled substance in the United States, meaning it have a high potential for abuse and no medical use.
- **Today:** Drug development and bio-tech companies doing trials now
  - Given its history, LSD less likely to gain FDA approval/reschedule
  - Even if shown efficacious, more likely that an analog gets approved

Autistic Psychedelic Community

MDMA LEGALITY

*MDMA is a federally illegal Schedule I substance in USA with a **potential path** toward legalized, FDA-approved usage of MDMA-assisted therapy for treatment of PTSD by 2024*

- **1912:** MDMA first synthesized by a German pharmaceutical company, Merck, but it was not initially invented nor studied for its psychoactive properties

- **1970:** MDMA began to be used in a therapeutic context, particularly in the field of psychology, where it was thought to be helpful in facilitating communication and emotional processing.

  - **1985:** MDMA was classified as a Schedule I controlled substance — however, thanks to MAPS & other orgs, a rescheduling is likely by 2024.

KETAMINE LEGALITY

Ketamine is a Schedule III FDA-approved medicine in the USA; although the substance has not been approved specifically for depression/suicidality, ketamine is available for off-label use

- **1960:** Ketamine was first synethesized by the pharmaceutical company Johnson & Johnson, which initially researched the drug as an anesthetic.

- **1980:** Johnson & Johnson stopped its research on ketamine as a treatment for depression due to concerns about the drug's potential for abuse.

  - **Today:** Although ketamine lacks direct indication by FDA for depression, J&J's recently approved esketamine (the S enantiomer of ketamine) has been approved and often given in conjunction with oral antidepressants.

AYAHUASCA LEGALITY

Ayahuasca is technically unscheduled but the DMT within the brew remains an illegal Schedule I substance in the USA

- For centuries, ayahuasca has been used by indigenous Amazonian cultures for spiritual and medicinal purposes.

- In recent decades, increasing awareness of ayahuasca has expanded around the world through journalism, media, etc.

- Today, ayahuasca is not approved for medical use by regulatory agencies such as the U.S. Food and Drug Administration (FDA), but is still available in certain protected religious / ceremonial contexts. More about access status for all of these compounds in Session III....

Currently Legal Psychedelic Options

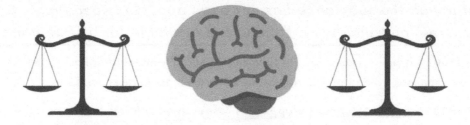

— Legal Points of Access in The USA & Abroad —

Autistic Psychedelic Community

 ## Decrim Vs. Legalization

"Decriminalizing" refers to reducing or eliminating criminal penalties for the possession and use of a particular drug

---

NOTE: decrim does not necessarily mean that the drug is legal, but rather that individuals who are caught with the drug may face civil fines or alternative penalties, such as treatment or education, rather than criminal charges, or merely protections provided at the state and/or local level.

 ## Decrim Vs. Legalization

"Legalizing" refers to making the drug available for legal use, possession, and/or sale, with some restrictions based on supervision.

NOTE: Legalizing a substance typically involves establishing regulations for the production, distribution, and sale. This typically occurs in an effort to generate tax revenue through the sale and regulation of the drug, and it may also reduce the costs associated with enforcing drug laws.

AUTISTIC
PSYCHEDELIC

Autistic Psychedelic Community

Clinical Trial Access

"Clinical Trials" for psychedelic medicine are conducted to evaluate the safety and efficacy of a new treatment or intervention.

There are a number of ways to locate clinical trials for psychedelic medicine, including through online resources such as ClinicalTrials.gov or the website of the National Institute on Drug Abuse (NIDA). To meet the requirements of a clinical trial, participants typically need to undergo various assessments and then follow specific treatment protocols.

Ketamine Clinics

"Ketamine Clinics" are healthcare facilities that offer ketamine-assisted therapy that is legal and covered by insurance in some cases.

NOTE: Ketamine is also available through emerging at-home services which provides lozenges pre-dosed and supplied to users who are then monitored remotely either via teleheath or with the direct assistance of a pre-approved support partner such as a housemate or family member.

Autistic Psychedelic Community

Entheogenic Access

"Entheogenic Access" refers to the use of psychedelics and plant medicines made possible by protections offered to spiritual or religious use.

In some countries and states, entheogrenic protections may allow for the use of certain psychedelics and plant medicines by members of indigenous or traditional spiritual practices, or by members of recognized religious organizations, or by visitors who visit to such organizations and become members.

Entheogenic Access

Entheogenic Access varies widely across the world and can also sometimes be "grey", but...some examples include...

- **The União do Vegetal:** Brazilian-based spiritual organization allowed to use ayahuasca for religious purposes in several countries in North America & EU

- **Santo Daime Church**: Another Brazilian-based spiritual organization that is allowed to use ayahuasca for religious purposes in North America/Europe

- **The Native American Church:** Native American spiritual organization allowed to use peyote for religious purposes in the United States and Canada.

  - **Various Latin America/Carribean Nations**: some spiritual practices that involve certain medicines, such as aya or psilocybin mushrooms, may be protected by local or national laws — again, it can be "grey"

 ## International Access

International Access also varies, and it remains EXTREMELY rare to see classical psychedelics fully legal for retail sale

- **Jamaica:** Psilocybin mushrooms are NOT banned in Jamaica and NOT listed as a controlled substance in the country's Dangerous Drugs Act (grey-market)

- **Netherlands:** Psychedelic drugs — including psilocybin truffles, cacti, and certain forms of DMT — are widely available at smart shops in the Netherlands. Whole fruiting body Psilocybe cubensis mushrooms, pure extractions, as well as ayahuasca remain illegal in the Netherlands — even for religious use.

  - **Canada**: In spite of illegality and shutdowns, various "dispensaries" continue to open in Canada selling just about every psychedelic drug known to man — LSD, DMT, 2-CB, coca, etc. — with many raided recently

 ## International Access

Additional examples of *International Access* include...

- **Costa Rica:** Psychedelic possession/use is not specifically illegal in CR

- **Mexico:** Psychedelic possession/use is not specifically illegal in Mexico, and ayahuasca in religious ceremonies is protected under freedom of religion right

- **Portugal**: ALL drug possession/use, including psychedelics, is decriminalized

- **Poland:** Psychedelic possession/use not specifically illegal

- **Peru:** Ayahuasca is legal for use in traditional ceremonies throughout country

  - **Psilocybin-Specific Access:** Austria (Illegal to Sell, Legal to Use), The Bahamas (Illegal to Sell, Legal to Use), Nepal (Legal to Use/Sell), Samoa (Illegal to Sell, Legal to Use), BVI (Illegal to Sell, Legal to Use)

Autistic Psychedelic Community

M109 in Oregon, USA

"*Oregon Measure 109*" allows for the regulation, licensing and administration of supervised psilocybin services in the state

How psilocybin products will get to a service center

1. Psilocybin products are cultivated, produced and/or processed by a licensed manufacturer. They are tracked in a product tracking system.

2. The products are tested by a licensed testing laboratory. The lab must be accredited by the Oregon Environmental Laboratory Accreditation Program (ORELAP). The test results are entered into the product tracking system.

3. The products are sold or transferred from a licensed manufacturer to a licensed service center. This is tracked in the product tracking system.

— M109 images courtesy of Oregon.gov/psilocybin

M109 in Oregon, USA

"*Oregon Measure 109*" recommends a 3-step process wherein facilitators meet for preparation, administration, and integration

How a client will access psilocybin services

 1. Preparation session: The client meets with a licensed facilitator for a preparation session.

 2. Administration session: The client consumes the product at the service center and begins their session with a licensed facilitator.

 3. Integration session: The client can take part in an optional session to follow up with a licensed facilitator and learn about additional peer support and other resources.

To provide these services, a licensed facilitator must complete:

- A training program with curriculum approved by OPS

- An exam administered by OPS, and

- All other license requirements.

— M109 images courtesy of Oregon.gov/psilocybin

 ## M109 in Oregon, USA

"Oregon Measure 109" has specific requirements for those who intend to become licensed facilitators in the state of Oregon...

Licensed Facilitator Requirements:

1) Must be 21 years of age or older.

2) Must have a high school diploma or equivalent.

3) Must be an Oregon resident (please note, this requirement expires in 2025).

4) Must pass a criminal background check.

5) Must complete a psilocybin facilitator training program with a curriculum approved by Oregon Psilocybin Services prior to applying for licensure.

6) Must pass an exam administered by Oregon Psilocybin Services.

— M109 images courtesy of Oregon.gov/psilocybin

  ## Prop 122 in Colorado, USA

"Colorado Prop 122" allows for the regulation, licensing and administration of supervised psilocybin services as of 2025

- **Funding:** Measure establishes a revenue fund to support the implementation and administration of the regulated access program

- **Similarity to Oregon 109:** The measure allows for the eventual issuance of natural medicine service provider licenses to qualified individuals in 2025

- **Going Beyond Oregon 109**: Prop 122 is a two-part measure. In addition to regulating a supervised psilocybin program, the measure decriminalizes cultivation, possession, use, sharing of "necessary' amount of the following: psilocybin, ibogaine, DMT, and mescaline (as long as it's not from peyote)

  - **After 2025:** Supervised use of other "natural meds" *might* be legalized if further research/public safety data supports legalizing supervised use

Autistic Psychedelic Community

"The State of Psy-Aut Care"
— Currently Unfolding Research —

Relevant Research/Readings

"AUTISM & PSYCHEDELICS - EXPLORING THE EXPERIENCES OF PSYCHEDELIC USE IN AUTISTIC PEOPLE"

Stroud et al (currently in peer review, publish expected 2023)

Scan to View Paper

Autistic Psychedelic Community

 "AUTISM & PSYCHEDELICS - EXPLORING THE EXPERIENCES OF PSYCHEDELIC USE IN AUTISTIC PEOPLE"

Study Design

- Naturalistic (use outside clinical context) survey collaboration between University College London + Autistic Psychedelic Community

- Examines relationships between scores of Autistic Quotient (AQ), Mystical Experience Questionnaire (MEQ), and Challenging Experiences Questionnaire (CEQ)

- Criteria: individuals must have been at least 18 years old and diagnosed with autism by a professional or self-identify as autistic, *and* must have used at least one psychedelic, MDMA, or ketamine.

SOURCE: HTTPS://AUTISTICPSYCHEDELIC.COM/SURVEYS

"AUTISM & PSYCHEDELICS - EXPLORING THE EXPERIENCES OF PSYCHEDELIC USE IN AUTISTIC PEOPLE"

Study Progress

- Paper has been submitted for peer review with intention to publish in open access scientific journal

- Cannot comment specifically on outcomes but basic preview is that autistics reported similar general health benefits seen in other similar surveys conducted in general adult populations

- Additional language analysis study presently also underway to examine text-box responses submitted during initial survey, with publish likely by 2024...

SOURCE: HTTPS://AUTISTICPSYCHEDELIC.COM/SURVEYS

AutisticPsychedelic.com

"SEROTONIN BRAIN NETWORKS IN AUTISTIC VERSUS NON-AUTISTIC ADULTS: AN EXPLORATORY DOUBLE-BLIND, RANDOMIZED, PLACEBO-CONTROLLED STUDY"

McAlonan et al (study underway, results expected by 2024)

Scan to View Paper

"SEROTONIN BRAIN NETWORKS IN AUTISTIC VERSUS NON-AUTISTIC ADULTS: AN EXPLORATORY DOUBLE-BLIND, RANDOMIZED, PLACEBO-CONTROLLED STUDY"

Study Design

- COMPASS Pathways is funding a study to investigate the effects of psilocybin on the brain pathways of autistic adults

- The double-blind, placebo-controlled study will compare function of serotonin brain networks in autistic and non-autistic adults

- The study will use a range of imaging techniques and behavioral tasks to examine how psilocybin impacts the serotonin system

  ○ Study is conducted at the Institute of Psychiatry, Psychology & Neuroscience at King's College London and co-sponsored by South London and Maudsley NHS Foundation Trust

SOURCE: HTTPS://CLINICALTRIALS.GOV/CT2/SHOW/NCT05651126

Autistic Psychedelic Community

"SEROTONIN BRAIN NETWORKS IN AUTISTIC VERSUS NON-AUTISTIC ADULTS: AN EXPLORATORY DOUBLE-BLIND, RANDOMIZED, PLACEBO-CONTROLLED STUDY"

Study Design

- The study will enroll 70 participants, including 40 autistic individuals and 30 non-autistic individuals.

- The study aims to improve understanding of the role of the serotonin system in autism and potentially identify new treatment options for autistic individuals.

- The company is developing a new model of psilocybin therapy using its proprietary formulation of synthetic psilocybin, COMP360, which has already been designated a Breakthrough Therapy by FDA for treatment-resistant depression

  - Study is currently in progress with results coming soon

  SOURCE: HTTPS://CLINICALTRIALS.GOV/CT2/SHOW/NCT05651126

Relevant Research/Readings

"A COMPARATIVE PHARMACOKINETICS & PHARMACODYNAMIC CLINICAL TRIAL OF R(-)-MDMA, S(+)-MDMA & R/S-MDMA IN A DOUBLE-BLIND, PLACEBO-CONTROLLED, CROSSOVER STUDY IN HEALTHY SUBJECTS"

(Liechti et al / Study currently in progress)

Scan to View Paper

AutisticPsychedelic.com

Autistic Psychedelic Community

Study Design

- MindMed is launching a program to develop R(-)-MDMA for the treatment of social anxiety and functioning in diagnoses including Autism Spectrum Disorder.

- R(-)-MDMA is thought to maintain pro-social and empathogenic benefits of racemic MDMA, while having fewer signs of stimulant activity, neurotoxicity, hyperthermia, and abuse liability.

- 24 healthy subjects each will receive R-MDMA (125 and 250mg), S-MDMA (125mg), MDMA (125mg), and placebo by end of study.

  - Preclinical studies suggest R-MDMA may have fewer adverse effects/greater prosocial effects

    SOURCE: HTTPS://MINDMED.CO/NEWS/PRESS-RELEASE/MINDMED-EXPANDS-ITS-DRUG-DEVELOPMENT-PIPELINE-WITH-LAUNCH-OF-R-MDMA-PROGRAM/

Relevant Research/Readings

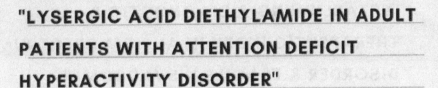

"LYSERGIC ACID DIETHYLAMIDE IN ADULT PATIENTS WITH ATTENTION DEFICIT HYPERACTIVITY DISORDER"

(Liechti et al / study currently in phase 2A)

Scan to View Paper

Autistic Psychedelic Community

Study Design

- MindMed has initiated Phase 2a proof-of-concept trial of LSD in adult patients w/ attention deficit hyperactivity disorder (ADHD)

- The trial will enroll a total of 52 patients that will receive 20µg of MM-120 (LSD-analogue) or placebo for 6 weeks

- The primary endpoint is the mean change from baseline in ADHD symptoms after 6 weeks of treatment

- The trial is designed to evaluate the tolerability therapeutic utility of low doses of MM-120; results are expected by 2024

SOURCE: HTTPS://CLINICALTRIALS.GOV/CT2/SHOW/NCT05200936

Relevant Research/Readings

"ESTABLISHING A DIAGNOSTIC & THERAPEUTIC INDEX IN AUTISM SPECTRUM DISORDER & FRAGILE X SYNDROME"

(Buzzelli et al / study currently in phase II)

Scan to View Paper

Autistic Psychedelic Community

"ESTABLISHING A DIAGNOSTIC & THERAPEUTIC INDEX IN AUTISM SPECTRUM DISORDER & FRAGILE X SYNDROME"

Study Design

- Fragile X syndrome (FXS) is common form of inherited intellectual disability and a leading cause of autism spectrum disorder (ASD)

- Serotonergic neurotransmission is important for normal brain development and has been linked to ASD and FXS.

- Psilocybin, a compound that stimulates serotonergic signaling, may be effective as an early intervention for developmental disorders such as ASD and FXS.

- The aim of the study was to determine if psilocybin could mitigate cognitive deficits in a rat model of ASD and FXS.

SOURCE: HTTPS://LINK.SPRINGER.COM/ARTICLE/10.1007/S00213-022-06286-3

"ESTABLISHING A DIAGNOSTIC & THERAPEUTIC INDEX IN AUTISM SPECTRUM DISORDER & FRAGILE X SYNDROME"

Phase I Outcomes

- Study found psilocybin administered orally or systemically normalized aberrant (narrow/rigid) cognitive performance in rat model.

- These findings support the hypothesis that serotonin-modulating drugs like psilocybin may be useful in addressing ASD-related cognitive challenges.

- The study provides evidence of the benefits of psilocybin in mitigating short-term cognitive challenges in a rat model of FXS.

SOURCE: HTTPS://LINK.SPRINGER.COM/ARTICLE/10.1007/S00213-022-06286-3

The Future of Psy-Aut Care

— Forecastable Psychedelic Autism Services —

 ## MDMA for PTSD

MDMA-Assisted Psychotherapy is forecasted to be approved by the FDA by Q4, 2023, after Phase 3b results are reviewed.

- Researchers to submit drug app for MDMA as a PTSD treatment by 2024.

- The US Food and Drug Administration may make a decision on approval within six months of receiving the application.

- If approved, MDMA could potentially be available in US hospitals — & potentially covered by insurance as a treatment for PTSD — by 2024.

  - Data varies, but a recent study found the probability of PTSD in UK autistic individuals was 35-42% as opposed to 4.5% in general pop**

**Source: https://www.autism.org.uk/advice-and-guidance/professional-practice/ptsd-autism

Autistic Psychedelic Community

 ## MDMA for PTSD in ASD

MDMA-Assisted Psychotherapy may be of interest to autistic individuals who can be prone to PTSD from various factors...

- **Potential Contributing Factors:**
  - Sensory experiences (even those labeled as "everyday" occurrences)
  - Transitions and change (trait listed as challenging for autistics)
  - Sustained state of social challenge and/or confusion
  - Detailed-focused mindset (ruminating on details vs processing situations)
  - Emotion regulation difficulties (shutdowns, meltdowns, dissociation)

Source: https://www.autism.org.uk/advice-and-guidance/professional-practice/ptsd-autism

 ## MDMA for PTSD in ASD

MDMA-Assisted Psychotherapy has the potential to help autistics & therapists overcome various barriers to treatment...

- **Alexithymia:** Difficulty labeling/identifying feelings in order to process them
  - (50-70% of autistics experience alexithymia**)
  - MDMA being an "entactogen" enhances awareness/retrieval
- **Social Exhaustion:** Interaction in general can more easily fatigue autistics
  - MDMA has stimulant effect, extending processing window/energy
- **Mistrust of Others:** Autistics may be more prone to distrust/vigilant response
  - MDMA shown to catalyze trust/bonds & elevate openness
  - Therapist-patient bond often strongest predictor of success

**Source: https://www.nature.com/articles/s41598-021-81696-5

 ## MDMA for PTSD in ASD

Additional Readings Related to ASD + Trauma

- **Does Autism Raise the Risk of PTSD?**

  https://www.scientificamerican.com/article/does-autism-raise-the-risk-of-ptsd/

 ## MDMA for Social Anxiety

MDMA-Assisted Psychotherapy has the potential to help autistics & therapists alleviate social anxiety disorder (SAD)...

- There is a **high overlap between ASD and social anxiety disorder**, with one review estimating that 50% of individuals with ASD met criteria for SAD compared to 7-13% of non-ASD population**

- Social anxiety in individuals with ASD may go undiagnosed due to a lack of awareness and difficulties with self-reporting.

- The pursuit of social anxiety treatment is inherently challenging as the very act avoiding social encounters is counter to the social model of therapy

**Source: Social Anxiety in Autism Spectrum Disorder: A Systematic Review
https://doi.org/10.1016/j.rasd.2018.04.007

Autistic Psychedelic Community

 ## MDMA for Social Anxiety

MDMA-Assisted Psychotherapy may be of interest to autistic individuals who can be prone to SAD from various factors...

- **Potential Contributing Factors:**
  - Difficulty processing social interactions and communication
  - Enduring sensory environments common in group gatherings
  - Stereotyped and idiosyncratic speech or preferences for discussing circumscribed interests may affect the fluidity of conversation
  - Repetitive behaviours or "stims" may appear odd to unaware others
  - Susceptibility to social adversity, e.g. rejection, teasing or bullying

**Source: Social Anxiety in Autism Spectrum Disorder: A Systematic Review
https://doi.org/10.1016/j.rasd.2018.04.007

 ## MDMA for Social Anxiety

MDMA-Assisted Psychotherapy has potential to help autistics & therapists overcome various barriers to SAD treatment......

- **Critical Periods:** MDMA has shown potential to re-open "critical periods" (CP)
  - Autistics may be withdrawn *in vivo*, resulting in less opportunity to learn social norms and augment social knowledge as children
  - If CP can be re-opened, second chances are possible for adults
- **Social Exhaustion:** Interaction in general can more easily fatigue autistics
  - MDMA has stimulant effect, extending processing window/energy
- **Continuation of CP After Session:** Potential for real world applications
  - Days after dosing, re-opened CP may allow for "neuro-rehab"

**Source: https://www.nature.com/articles/s41598-021-81696-5

 Of Mice & MDMA

- Dölen et al studied social reward learning in mice in enclosures with different bedding

- Mice were first put together in one enclosure with one type of bedding for 24 hours

- In next 24 hours, same mice were solo into an enclosure with a different type of bedding

- The mice began to associate certain types of bedding with isolation or companionship

- Then, researchers let the mice wander between enclosures with the two types of bedding and tracked how long the mice spent in each enclosure

- More time mice spent in bedding linked to companions indicated social reward learning

- Following MDMA treatment, mice given MDMA responded to social interactions similarly to juveniles, forming a positive association between social interactions and bedding

- This effect lasted at least 2 weeks & not observed in mice given saline solution

Source: https://hopkinsmedicine.org/news/newsroom/news-releases/psychedelic-drug-mdma-may-reawaken-critical-period-in-brain-to-help-treat-ptsd

Supervised Psilo in OR

Supervised Psilocybin Sessions are forecasted to be available in Oregon in Q2/Q3, 2023, giving therapists new adjunct tools.

- It will still take some time for all four license types (manufacturing, testing, service centers, and facilitators) to be established and begin operations.

- Oregon residency is not required for your clients to access psilocybin services

- Adults 21+ can access supervised psilocybin sessions for any reason as long as they complete preparation/screening/administration with licensed facilitator.

- Microdosing (doses containing <2.5 mg of psilocybin) will be allowed but recipient must be supervised at licensed center for stated minimums:
  - Low Dose: <2.5mg=30 min minimum /// 2.5mg-5mg=60 min minimum
  - High Dose: 35mg-50mg (max allowed per session) = 6 hour minimum

Source: https://oregon.gov/psilocybin/

The Future of Psy-Aut Care

— *Theoretical Psychedelic Autism Services* —

 ## Interoception Training

Interoception Training *is a more recently developed approach that focused on establishing agency through somatic awareness*

- Typically administered by an occupational therapist, this work involves teaching individuals with autism spectrum disorder ASD to recognize and interrupt unwanted sensations and patterns before they escalate

- May be helpful for individuals with ASD as it can help them to develop greater self-awareness and identify triggers that lead to negative thoughts, sensations, behaviors, or other poor mental health outcomes

- Interception training may also improve basic physical health in individuals with ASD as it can help aid basic self-care routines and practices (e.g., noticing hunger sensations and then actually eating)

 Interoception Training

Interoception Training could potentially be enhanced through augmentation with low doses of psychedelics like psilocybin

- **Increased Emotional Regulation:** Psilocybin has been shown to enhance emotional regulation, allowing individuals to better manage their emotions and physical sensations. (Lebedev et al., 2017)

- **Enhanced Perception of Bodily Sensations:** Psilocybin has been shown to enhance perception of bodily sensations, leading to increased attention and awareness of internal states. (Roseman et al., 2017)

  - **Improved Sensory Integration:** Psilocybin has been shown to improve sensory integration, leading to better regulation of sensory input and more coherent perception of bodily sensations. (Schmid et al., 2015)

 Psychedelic Social Skills Groups

Social Skills Groups aim to help autistic individuals improve their interactions and communication skills via group learning

- Sessions typically involve practicing and role-playing different social situations, such as starting conversations, making eye contact, and expressing emotions appropriately in accordance with a given context

- Conventional social skills trainings involve teaching individuals with autism about neurotypical "norms and expectations", but this is being re-thought

- In autistic-majority-spaces, new possibilities for "neuro-rehabilitation" arise — opportunities to normalize "less common social approaches" like parallel play, or the use of adaptive technologies such as text-to-speech or live transcript devices, ear/eye protection, etc.

 Psychedelic Occupational Therapy

Occupational Therapy helps autistics with activities they want/need to do via therapeutic use of "occupations"

- "Occupations" refer to everyday activities that bring meaning and purpose to life
- Occupational therapists work with people who have physical, mental, or social challenges that make it hard for them to do things they want or need to do.
- Occupational therapists use a variety of approaches to help people develop, recover, or maintain the skills needed for daily living and work.
- Occupational therapists use a variety of approaches to help people develop, recover, or maintain the skills needed for daily living and work
- Psychedelic-assisted OT would hypothetically involve low-dose psilo/LSD
- For example applications, see next slide....

 Psychedelic Occupational Therapy

Occupational Therapy encompasses a wide range of approaches — some example approaches include...

- **Sensory Integration Therapy:** Using sensory activities to help the individual regulate their responses to sensory input and develop coping strategies.
- **Play-Based Therapy**: Encouraging social interaction/communication via play
- **Fine and Gross Motor Skill Development**: Improving coordination, strength, and dexterity through targeted exercises and activities.
- **Adaptive Skills Training:** Teaching self-care, domestic, and community skills to help the individual become more independent.
- **Environmental Modifications and Exploration:** Considering changes to individual's physical environment to make it more conducive to their needs.

Autistic Psychedelic Community

 Psychedelic Occupational Therapy

Occupational Therapy could potentially be augmented by low doses of psilocybin/LSD to potentially enhance outcomes...

- **Increased Creativity and Problem-Solving Ability:** Psilocybin has been shown to increase creativity and problem-solving, leading to improved performance in occupational therapy activities requiring these skills. (Carhart-Harris et al., 2014)

- **Improved Mood and Emotional Regulation:** Psilocybin has been shown to improve mood and emotional regulation, leading to decreased symptoms of depression and anxiety and a greater ability to participate in occupational therapy activities. (Lebedev et al., 2017; Garcia-Romeu et al., 2014)

- **Enhanced Self-Awareness and Introspection:** Psilocybin has been shown to enhance self-awareness/introspection, leading to improved communication /understanding between patient and therapist. (Carhart-Harris et al., 2014)

 Psychedelic Cognitive-Behavioral Therapy

Cognitive Behavioral Therapy focuses on the relationships between thoughts/feelings/behaviors...Examples include:

- **Cognitive Restructuring:** Examining and challenging negative thoughts and beliefs and replacing one's self with more "balanced and rational" thoughts — *could be enhanced by "divergent thinking enhancements" of psilocybin*

- **Behavioural Techniques:** Learning and practicing new coping skills and behavior strategies, such as relaxation techniques, with the therapist — *could be enhanced through increased somatic access of psilocybin*

- **Exposure Therapy:** Gradually facing and learning to manage fear-inducing situations or thoughts through repeated exposure — *could be enhanced by the fear-response-lowering nature of MDMA-assisted therapy environment*

Psychedelic Family Therapy

Psychedelic Family Therapy seeks to also address the impacts of autistic challenges on the mental health of whole families

- Psychedelic Family Therapy takes into account social model of disability and honors challenges that all members may face, creating space for forgiveness, self-forgiveness, and the engagement of otherwise abandoned discussions

- In autism specifically, the likelihood of overlapping trait presentation within genetic pools is elevated, potentially compounding challenges that could therefore be addressed in an inclusive, family-facing context

- Conducting this work adjacent to therapist support likely most efficacious

- Obvious Catch: Therapeutic psychedelic work for multiple individuals is inherently more costly with exponentially more risk of adverse response

Psychedelic Family Therapy

Psychedelic Family Therapy addresses various challenges families may face while raising autistic individuals, including...

- **Stress and Exhaustion:** Caring for an autistic individual can be physically and emotionally demanding, and can lead to increased levels of stress and exhaustion for parents and siblings

- **Social Isolation:** Parents and siblings of an autistic individual may experience social isolation due to time and energy required to care for the child, as well as the challenges of navigating social activities with an autistic individual

- **Guilt and Blame:** Parents and siblings may experience feelings of guilt or blame, either for the challenges they've faced in their own life or for feelings of frustration or difficulty in coping with challenges of advocating and supporting autistic individuals over the course of their lifetimes

 Psychedelic Support Partner Sessions

Psychedelic Support Partner Sessions *are primarily supported by a sober, familiar parter—and secondarily supported by a therapist/EMT*

- Mirrors model seen in some forms of at-home ketamine lozenge therapy work

- Support partner receives basic space holding and active listening training and then "sits" with recipient during the session while qualified practitioner remains within contact either on-site or via remote emergency contact

- Would likely be used in low-dose work to reduce challenges/adverse outcomes

- Some concerns regarding whether or not this might put an individual into a vulnerable position; e.g., medicine recipient is in abusive relationship and becomes aware of this during a session with the partner — can be triggering.

- Set & setting is still an essential consideration, and the adjunct of having a third-party therapist would also likely help to enhance outcomes

 Psychedelic Immersion Therapy

Psychedelic Immersion Therapy *involves the consumption of a take-home psychedelic in "naturalistic" or "real world" contexts*

- "Immersion" refers to being in familiar, supervised or unsupervised settings

- Primary advantage of real-world immersion therapy is that the invidual succeeds in an environment that is relevant, meaningful, and highly practical

- Additional benefit is that such environments might feel more safe or secure than more sterile/medical environments, or more foreign settings like retreats

- If unsupervised, inherent risks become the potential suggestibility of the user, the unpredictability of situation, and/or uncontrollable nature of surroundings

- Maximum attention to set and setting would likely lead to optimal outcomes

 Psychedelic Immersion Therapy

Psychedelic Immersion Therapy would most likely involve microdoses/low doses that support public-facing functionality

- LSD microdoses could be taken in the morning and last up to 8 hours, supporting focus/attentiveness/sociability enhancements in the workplace or other context

- Psilocybin microdoses could serve similar role with "context-dependent" dosing

- Unparalleled Benefit: Participants get chance to revisit challenging situations (family gatherings, job interviews) with fresh eyes and perspective — as opposed to just talking about situations in a therapetic office or role-playing context

- Personal Aside: I wrote extensively about this in my book, "Autism On Acid", and I feel that no other form of conventional herapy would have brought me to this place of growth... I was able to "walk through the electric fence of conditioning" and build confidence... I could actually *walk the walk* instead of *just* talk....

"The Future of Psy-Aut Care"
— *Accommodation Considerations* —

Autistic Psychedelic Community

 ## ND-Friendly Intake Questions

ND-Friendly Intake Questions can enhance comfort and clarity before, during, and after intentional psychedelic sessions. Here's some examples:

- Do you have any personal comfort objects you would prefer have in session?
- Do you have sensitivities to any of the following?
  - Light
  - Sounds
  - Scents
  - Texture/Touch
  - Other
- Which is easiest for you in terms of being able to process and recall?
  - When information is written down
  - When information is spoken

  ## Sensory-Based Accommodations

Sensory-Based Accommodations can be helpful for enhancing comfort, focus, and outcomes during psychedelic sessions. Here's some examples:

- **Visual Sensitivity Accommodations:**
  - Avoiding use of direct light/white light/flashing lights in the setting
  - Having sunglasses or eye blinds for clients to help reduce visual overwhelm
- **Sound Sensitivity Accommodations:**
  - Having noise cancelling headphones or ear defenders for clients to borrow
  - Providing "Loop" noise-reducing earplug devices to soften/dampen sounds
  - Avoiding white noise machines, fans, other repetitive environmental noise
  - Providing clients the ability to curate or pre-approve music playlists
- **Textures/Touch/Sensorimotor Accommodations**
  - Microfiber blankets, weighted blankets, squeezable plush objects
  - Stim toys, fidget spinners, pop-it rubber fidget devices

AutisticPsychedelic.com

Autistic Psychedelic Community

  Sensory-Based Accommodations

Processing-Related Accommodations *can be helpful for enhancing communications before, during, and after sessions. Here's some examples:*

- **Accommodating Auditory Processing Challenges:**
  - Providing written instructions or utilizing live transcription softwares
  - Allowing session audio to be recorded to be revisited and recalled
- **Accommodating Dyslexia/Reading Challenges:**
  - Using visual symbols whenever possible in spoken/written communications
  - Including clear, unbusy, minimalistic visual signage throughout the space
- **Accommodating Non-Verbal Clients:**
  - Allowing use of assistive communication devices
  - Offering option for text-message-based or written communications
  - Establishing agreed-upon gestures for more fluid communications
  - Example: simple raise of hand or cards to request restroom break

 Considerations Regarding Groups

Group Considerations *include any intentional choices that help to increase feelings of safety and comfort for a client...*

- **Honor The Comfort Level Regarding Groups:** Depending on the client, group psychedelic sessions can be perceived as *either* overwhelming or as opportunities to overcome social fears. Don't push it. There's always time.

- **Start With Small Victories And Build From There:** If dealing with a psychedelic-naïve client, allow them to familiarize themselves with the medicine first. Then consider group work. Then consider group medicine work.

  - **Provide As Much Abundance And Options As Possible:** Even if the clients do not utilize all of the options made available to them during a session, the mere providence of the options can be a comfort unto itself. For example, having a sufficient number of separate — but still supervised — quiet spaces for each participant can be helpful. Same for food options.

Autistic Psychedelic Community

 Provider Self-Assessment Worksheet

To further consider accommodations in your practice, it is suggested that you consider completing the following worksheet to assess the level of accommodation you're providing.

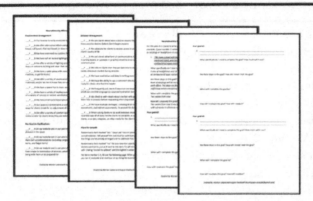

"Neurodiversity Accommodations Self-Assesment Worksheet" Created By ND-Affirming Specialists Worner Leland, MS, BCBA, LB & August Stockwell, PhD

This Full Worksheet Is Hosted As A Google Doc At The Following Link: TinyURL.com/ndselfassessment

Scan to View Paper

"The Future of Psy-Aut Care"
— Relevant / Of-The-Moment Research —

Autistic Psychedelic Community

"EFFECTS OF MDMA ON ATTENTION TO POSITIVE SOCIAL CUES & PLEASANTNESS OF AFFECTIVE TOUCH"

(Bershard et al, 2019)

Scan to View Paper

 "EFFECTS OF MDMA ON ATTENTION TO POSITIVE SOCIAL CUES & PLEASANTNESS OF AFFECTIVE TOUCH"

Study Summary

- The study investigated the effects of MDMA and MA (compared to placebo) on responses to affective touch and visual attention to emotional faces.

- Affective touch is a type of touch that evokes an emotional response. This type of touch involves skin-to-skin contact that is nurturing, caring, or affectionate, and can have a positive impact on our emotional well-being.

SOURCE: HTTPS://DOI.ORG/10.1038/S41386-019-0402-Z

"EFFECTS OF MDMA ON ATTENTION TO POSITIVE SOCIAL CUES & PLEASANTNESS OF AFFECTIVE TOUCH"

Study Outcomes

- Researchers found that MDMA seemed to affect the part of the brain responsible for processing affective touch.

- These results provide new evidence that MDMA can enhance the experience of positive social interactions; in this case, pleasantness of physical touch and attentional bias toward positive facial expressions.

  - Results support the theory that MDMA alters social behavior by changing serotonin and oxytocin signaling in the brain.

SOURCE: HTTPS://DOI.ORG/10.1038/S41386-019-0402-Z

Relevant Research/Readings

"MDMA-ASSISTED THERAPY AS A MEANS TO ALTER AFFECTIVE, COGNITIVE, BEHAVIORAL, AND NEUROLOGICAL SYSTEMS UNDERLYING SOCIAL DYSFUNCTION IN SOCIAL ANXIETY DISORDER"

(Luoma et al, 2021)

Scan to View Paper

Autistic Psychedelic Community

"MDMA-ASSISTED THERAPY AS A MEANS TO ALTER AFFECTIVE, COGNITIVE, BEHAVIORAL, AND NEUROLOGICAL SYSTEMS UNDERLYING SOCIAL DYSFUNCTION IN SOCIAL ANXIETY DISORDER"

Context of Review

- Paper highlights how people with SAD often perceive social situations as threatening and experience heightened activity in the amygdala (a brain region involved in emotion) in response to social threats or negative feedback.

- The social engagement system, which includes the parasympathetic nervous system and vagus nerve, helps regulate physiological arousal and facilitate responsive and flexible social interactions.

SOURCE: HTTPS://DOI.ORG/10.3389/FPSYT.2021.733893

"MDMA-ASSISTED THERAPY AS A MEANS TO ALTER AFFECTIVE, COGNITIVE, BEHAVIORAL, AND NEUROLOGICAL SYSTEMS UNDERLYING SOCIAL DYSFUNCTION IN SOCIAL ANXIETY DISORDER"

Review Findings

- People with SAD tend to have lower activity in the social engagement system, which can be seen in reduced heart rate variability and impaired ability to respond to social situations in a sensitive and synchronous manner.

- Dysfunctional interpersonal behaviors, such as avoidance and safety behaviors, can interfere with social functioning and close relationships in SAD.

- Heightened shame and rigid use of shame regulation strategies may also contribute to maintenance of SAD.

SOURCE: HTTPS://DOI.ORG/10.3389/FPSYT.2021.733893

Autistic Psychedelic Community

"MDMA-ASSISTED THERAPY AS A MEANS TO ALTER AFFECTIVE, COGNITIVE, BEHAVIORAL, AND NEUROLOGICAL SYSTEMS UNDERLYING SOCIAL DYSFUNCTION IN SOCIAL ANXIETY DISORDER"

Implications for MDMA

- MDMA has been shown to affect the social engagement system by increasing heart rate variability, enhancing feelings of safety and connection, and increasing activity in vagus nerve.

- The effects of MDMA on the social engagement system may extend beyond the acute dosing period, potentially helping to alter the balance of approach vs avoidance goals in social situations that maintain SAD.

- Therefore, MDMA may improve social skills, increase feelings of belonging and acceptance, and enhance social efficacy.

SOURCE: HTTPS://DOI.ORG/10.3389/FPSYT.2021.733893

Relevant Research/Readings

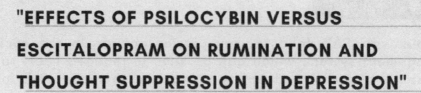

"EFFECTS OF PSILOCYBIN VERSUS ESCITALOPRAM ON RUMINATION AND THOUGHT SUPPRESSION IN DEPRESSION"

(Barba et al, 2022)

Scan to
View Paper

"EFFECTS OF PSILOCYBIN VERSUS ESCITALOPRAM ON RUMINATION AND THOUGHT SUPPRESSION IN DEPRESSION"

Study Design

- This study sought assess the comparative effect of psilocybin and escitalopram (SSRI) on rumination and thought suppression.

- Study had a total of six weeks (prep, administration, integration, administration, integration, optional integration on week 6)

- After administration sessions, participants got take-home capsules (of either ssri or placebo) to take daily, each morning,

SOURCE:HTTPS://DOI.ORG/10.1192/BJO.2022.565

"EFFECTS OF PSILOCYBIN VERSUS ESCITALOPRAM ON RUMINATION AND THOUGHT SUPPRESSION IN DEPRESSION"

Psilocybin (n=30)	Day	Escitalopram (n=29)	
Baseline visit/measures: rumination (RRS), thought suppression (WBSI), depression (QIDS-SR-16)	−7	Baseline visit/measures: rumination (RRS), thought suppression (WBSI), depression (QIDS-SR-16)	
Preparation session		Preparation session	
Dosing day 1: 25 mg of psilocybin, placebo capsules for 3 weeks; completion of acute measures (EDI, EBI, CEQ)	0	Dosing day 1: 1 mg of psilocybin, 10 mg of escitalopram for 3 weeks; completion of acute measures (EDI, EBI, CEQ)	🍄 1MG +
Integration session 1	1	Integration session 2	SSRI – 10MG X 21 DAYS
Dosing day 2: 25 mg of psilocybin, placebo capsules for 3 weeks; completion of acute measures (EDI, EBI, CEQ)	21	Dosing day 2: 1 mg of psilocybin, 20 mg of escitalopram for 3 weeks; completion of acute measures (EDI, EBI, CEQ)	🍄 1MG +
Integration session 2	22	Integration session 2	SSRI – 20MG X 21 DAYS
6-week follow-up: debriefing, completion of subjective measures (RRS, WBSI, QIDS-SR-16, PIS-6)	42	6-week follow-up: debriefing, completion of subjective measures (RRS, WBSI, QIDS-SR-16, PIS-6)	

🍄 **25MG PSILO +**

PLACEBO X 21 DAYS

🍄 **25MG PSILO +**

PLACEBO X 21 DAYS

SOURCE:HTTPS://DOI.ORG/10.1192/BJO.2022.565

Autistic Psychedelic Community

Results Summary

- Psilocybin responders showed significant reductions in domains of both rumination and thought suppression, whereas the escitalopram responders only showed reductions in rumination,

- Because a "reduction in thought suppression" actually means that thoughts could still be processed, the theory goes that psilocybin might afford relief from rumination while still allowing for the processing of insights amidst integrative therapy sessions

- Key Limitation: 6-week duration may not reveal full effect of SSRI / psilo intervention outcome measures as compared to established evidence-based efficacy of such compounds...

SOURCE:HTTPS://DOI.ORG/10.1192/BJO.2022.565

Relevant Research/Readings

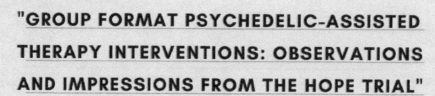

"GROUP FORMAT PSYCHEDELIC-ASSISTED THERAPY INTERVENTIONS: OBSERVATIONS AND IMPRESSIONS FROM THE HOPE TRIAL"

(Lewis et al, 2023)

Scan to View Paper

"GROUP FORMAT PSYCHEDELIC-ASSISTED THERAPY INTERVENTIONS:
OBSERVATIONS AND IMPRESSIONS FROM THE HOPE TRIAL"

Study Design

- Within clinical research, group therapy studies of classic psychedelics like psilocybin are rare and in need of investigation

- This study recruited individuals with DSM-5 depressive disorder who also had an underlying cancer diagnosis

- Following screening, 4-6 participants per cohort (with three total cohorts) were enrolled in a protocol involving three 120-min group preparatory sessions, a single high-dose (25 mg) group psilocybin session, and 3 subsequent group integration sessions.

- Qualitative reports were then gathered with responses to the following five survey questions...

SOURCE: HTTPS://DOI.ORG/10.1556/2054.2022.00222

"GROUP FORMAT PSYCHEDELIC-ASSISTED THERAPY INTERVENTIONS:
OBSERVATIONS AND IMPRESSIONS FROM THE HOPE TRIAL"

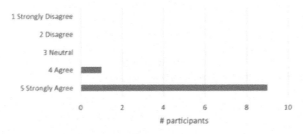

I felt like the group format psilocybin session worked well and maximized my individual therapeutic response

Mean score = 4.9

SOURCE: HTTPS://DOI.ORG/10.1556/2054.2022.00222

Autistic Psychedelic Community

I felt an increased connection to other group members
in virtue of having a group format psilocybin session
and having some contact with their individual
processes.

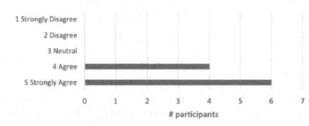

Mean score = 4.6

SOURCE: HTTPS://DOI.ORG/10.1556/2054.2022.00222

I felt like the group psilocybin session was a natural
extension of the group process initiated through the
preparatory sessions

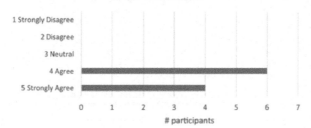

Mean score = 4.4

SOURCE: HTTPS://DOI.ORG/10.1556/2054.2022.00222

"GROUP FORMAT PSYCHEDELIC-ASSISTED THERAPY INTERVENTIONS: OBSERVATIONS AND IMPRESSIONS FROM THE HOPE TRIAL"

I felt like having a communal music track worked well.

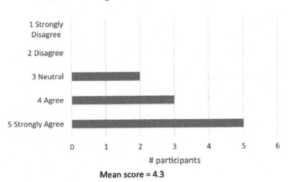

Mean score = 4.3

SOURCE: HTTPS://DOI.ORG/10.1556/2054.2022.00222

"GROUP FORMAT PSYCHEDELIC-ASSISTED THERAPY INTERVENTIONS: OBSERVATIONS AND IMPRESSIONS FROM THE HOPE TRIAL"

I would have preferred to have an individual music track with headphones for the psilocybin session.

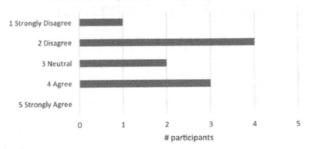

Mean score = 2.7

SOURCE: HTTPS://DOI.ORG/10.1556/2054.2022.00222

Autistic Psychedelic Community

Study Implications

- Study demonstrated that structure of group therapy can be not only cost-effective but also elevate outcomes in some cases

- Participants strongly agreed on the utility of group dynamic

- Participants had mixed response to ability to control music playlist or have their own separated auditory environment

- This is of particular interest to psilocybin group therapy for autistics, especially considering sound sensitivities, diversity of sound sensitivity profiles, and potentially heightened need for self-containment when entering into heightened/altered states

SOURCE: HTTPS://DOI.ORG/10.1556/2054.2022.00222

Relevant Research/Readings

"SUPPORT FOR ADULTS WITH AUTISM SPECTRUM DISORDER WITHOUT INTELLECTUAL IMPAIRMENT: SYSTEMATIC REVIEW"

(Lorenc et al, 2017)

Scan to
View Paper

Autistic Psychedelic Community

Review Highlights

- Review explored approaches to supporting autistic adults (social skills training, job interview training, employment support, music and dance, support and mentoring for students, safety training, and specialist multidisciplinary teams)

- Employment programs and social skills training were found to be among the most effective approaches studied in this review

- Most interventions focused on mitigating specific deficits rather than providing broader support

- More research is needed on the effectiveness of supportive interventions such as advocacy and mentoring for adults with ASD without intellectual impairment.

SOURCE: HTTPS://DOI.ORG/10.1177/1362361317698939

Relevant Research/Readings

FIRST-HAND PERSPECTIVES ON BEHAVIORAL INTERVENTIONS FOR AUTISTIC PEOPLE AND PEOPLE WITH OTHER DEVELOPMENTAL DISABILITIES

Autistic Self-Advocacy Network, 2017

There's so much more we could explore and discuss... But for now we'll take pause and leave you with the following report, in which autistic adults share openly about their own lived experiences in navigating existing autism care models. As you will see in this report, many issues still need to be addressed in present models of autism care (regardless of whether or not psychedelics are involved). And so we end this text with the reminder that no matter how we approach this work, we must always strive to (1) do no harm and (2) honor and center the agency of autistic individuals whenever possible.

Scan to View Paper

Source: AutisticAdvocacy.org/wp-content/uploads/2017/05/Behavioral-Interventions-Report-Final.pdf

Closing Thoughts

The information presented within this book has been offered as an early foundation upon which we can all build the future of psychedelic autism care, together. As stated in the introduction of this book, there are still many questions to be answered. And to be clear: anyone who is interested in pursuing this work is bound to still have questions as we continue carefully forward into this new frontier. As time goes on, more and more evidence will be gathered in both clinical and community-based contexts. And that's great. Because the information that we presently hold is merely the beginning of a lengthy exploration. Autism is spectral in nature. And the trait presentations and challenges that this field of care will be navigating will be likewise widely varied and unique unto themselves. As time goes on, the aim of the APC is to continue to serve as a central global meeting point for autistic individuals, family members, and the professionals who seek to serve them through a intentional and collaborative multidisciplinary approach. And it is through the publishing of books such as this that we hope to foster general awareness while at the same time welcoming critical dialogues to continue to unfold. In the world of autism care and psychedelics, there is no one golden standard of approach. Just as psychedelic medicines offer many different applications that can vary based on dose, mindset, context, and setting, so also does this global community offer a wide range of skills and abilities that will be useful at specific times, in specific contexts. In the coming years, many of the studies mentioned within this handbook will undergo peer review and publication. We will know more than we know today. And we will understand the mechanism of both psychedelics and autism in a much more nuanced and complete manner. And so the goal, at the present, is to simply invite readers like you to join this effort. In doing so, you'll help us all to better understand the safest and most efficacious approaches within psychedelic autism care. We know a lot now. And we're learning more every day. So please, join us as we continue on with this great, grand, global collaboration.

With Gratitude + Deep Appreciation For All Who've Contributed To This Effort,
— Aaron@AutisticPsychedelic.com

Suggested Reading

The foundational outlooks & insights presented in this book as well as other offerings created for AutisticPsychedelic.com would not have been possible without the following contributions from various educators, writers, doctors, researchers, and advocates...

The Adult Autism Assessment Handbook Paperback: A Neuro-Affirmative Approach
Davida Hartman, Tara O'Donnell-Killen, Jessica K Doyle,
Dr Maeve Kavanagh, Dr Anna Day, Dr Juliana Azevedo

Handbook of Medical Hallucinogens, 1st Edition
Dr Charles Grob + Jim Grigsby, PhD

Divergent Mind: Thriving In A World That Wasn't Designed For You
Jenera Nerenberg, PhD

Unmasking Autism: Discovering The New Faces of Neurodiversity
Devon Price, PhD

NeuroDiversity: The Birth Of An Idea
Judy Singer

**The Psychedelic Handbook: A Practical Guide To
Psilocybin, LSD, Ketamine, MDMA, And Ayahuasca**
Dr Rick Strassman

**Neuroqueer Heresies: Notes On The Neurodiversity Paradigm,
Autistic Empowerment, And Postnormal Possibilities**
Nick Walker, PhD

**Can Magic Mushrooms Unlock Depression?
What I've Learned In The Five Fears Since My TEDx Talk**
Dr Rosalind Watts (post available via Medium.com)

JOIN US FOR OUR WEEKLY OPEN ZOOM MEETING

EVERY SUNDAY
@11AM PST
/2PM EST

Autistic Psychedelic Community
AutisticPsychedelic.com

We Meet Live Online Every Sunday @ 11am PST

In Other Words...

Samoa	8am	
Hawaii/ Tahiti	9am	
Alaska	10am	
Pacific Time (US & Canada)	11am	
Arizona/ Mountain Time (US & Canada)	12pm	
Mexico City/ Central Time (US & Canada)	1pm	
Bogota/ Lima/ New York	2pm	**S**
La Paz/ San Juan/ Santiago	3pm	**U**
Brasilia/ Buenos Aires/ Montevideo	4pm	**N**
Mid-Atlantic	5pm	**D**
Azores/ Cape Verde Is	6pm	**A**
Dublin/ Lisbon/ London/ Reykjavik	7pm	**Y**
Amsterdam/ Berlin/ Paris/ Rome	8pm	
Bucharest/ Beirut/ Cairo/ Helsinki	9pm	
Baghdad/ Moscow/ Nairobi	10pm	
Dubai/ Abu Dhabi/ Muscat/ Baku/ Port Louis	11pm	
Islamabad/ Karachi/ Tashkent	12am	
Astana/ Dhaka/ Novosibirsk	1am	**M**
Bangkok/ Hanoi/ Jakarta	2am	**O**
Beijing/ Hong Kong/ Singapore	3am	**N**
Osaka/ Tokyo/ Seoul/ Yakutsk	4am	**D**
Canberra/ Melbourne/ Sydney	5am	**A**
Magadan/ Solomon Is.	6am	**Y**
Auckland/ Wellington/ Fiji	7am	

"**[ON PSYCHEDELICS]**, I HAD 1ST TIME EXPERIENCE OF BEING CALM, SAFE AND CERTAIN IN MY MIND. I LEARNED THAT I DON'T NEED TO CONTROL MY SENSORY EXPERIENCE TO STAY SANE —ACTUALLY, QUITE THE OPPOSITE."

— Jessica, Age 26 —
[Autistic / ADHD]

"**[LSD]** CAUSED ME TO REACT TO THIS INCREDIBLE AMOUNT OF HAPPINESS (WHICH I USUALLY HAVE TROUBLE EXPRESSING) BY SOBBING FROM HAPPINESS FOR THE FIRST TIME IN MY LIFE."

— Hannah, Age 20 —
[Asperger's Syndrome]

"I OWE MY LIFE TO THESE DRUGS. AND BECAUSE OF MY EXPERIENCES WITH PSYCHEDELICS, I AM A HAPPIER PERSON AND TO ME THAT IS WHY WE ARE ALL HERE: TO SHARE THIS EXPERIENCE; TO GROW; TO LOVE, TOGETHER."

— Bobby, Age 29 —
[Autistic]

"I WOULD NOT BE ABLE TO BE THE ORGANIZER I AM TODAY — NOR WOULD I HOLD THE INTENTION OF SERVING AS A HEALER IN THE FUTURE — WITHOUT MY RELATIONSHIP WITH PSYCHEDELICS. LIKE GRETA THUNBERG, I BELIEVE THAT AUTISM CAN BE A SUPERPOWER, & I AM SO GRATEFUL THAT I HAVE AN OPPORTUNITY TO DEVELOP MINE."

— Shae, Age 27 —
[Autistic]

"AFTER THIS PSYCHEDELIC EXPERIENCE, I WAS ABLE TO FINALLY CONNECT WITH MY THOUGHTS — AND WITH MYSELF — WITHOUT EXPERIENCING CONSTANT WORRY, SELF-CRITICISM, AND SHAME.

IN FEELING GOOD ABOUT MYSELF, I BECAME MORE CAPABLE OF APPRECIATING MYSELF AS I AM — AS COLORFUL, DIVERSE, VIBRANT ... LIKE A SPECTRUM."

— Gregory —
[Autistic Adult]

PSYCHEDELIC NEURO DIVERSITY

Stream It On **Spotify**

AN EPISODIC AUDIO DOC & PODCAST EXPLORING MEANINGFUL PSYCHEDELIC EXPERIENCES VIA THE VOICES OF NEURODIVERGENT STORYTELLERS

PRODUCED & PRESENTED BY
AUTISTICPSYCHEDELIC.COM

To listen to this podcast, please visit
AutisticPsychedelic.com/podcast

— Introduction to — Psychedelic Autism

An Online Course for Facilitators & Therapists

Join us for a first-of-a-kind webinar series exploring the past, present & future of psychedelic-assisted care options for autistic adults. Created with facilitators, therapists, guides, sitters & coaches in mind, this community offering includes lectures, a review of peer-reviewed reference materials, plus the chance to connect with other wellness practitioners. By the end of the course, enrollees will be better able to accommodate, understand, serve & support autistic adults within ceremonial, session-based, & coaching-related psychedelic contexts.

For Enrollment Info, Scan The Code Below or Visit AutisticPsychedelic.com/learn

AutisticPsychedelic.com/learn

Autistic Psychedelic Community

To connect with our community, please visit

www.AutisticPsychedelic.com

Visit Site   Contact Us

Autistic Psychedelic Community

Thank you once again to all those who've taken time to read through our books, or to listen to our podcasts, or attend our meetings, or contribute to our community's mission in any way. Our progress is the net result of thousands of helpful humans continuously offering whatever they can from all corners of the world. And by virtue of you simply educating yourself on what we do — & why we do it — you're already playing a helpful role in this global collaboration. If you'd like to collaborate further, we welcome you to send along an email or say hello at any of our online meetings. As stated in many of our previous books: there's a great big internet out there, & there's plenty of space for all of us to collaborate & connect, anytime, from anywhere on earth...

Thank you once again. It is an honor to be of service to this community.

With Gratitude,
Aaron@AutisticPsychedelic.com

P.S. - That's my email. Reach out anytime :)

Made in the USA
Columbia, SC
05 July 2023

20012187R10057